instant

RUSSIAN

Elisabeth Smith

TEACH YOURSELF BOOKS

The author would like to thank all the language consultants that helped in the preparation of this book.

There is a cassette (ISBN: 0 340 78106 8) available to accompany this book. If you experience problems obtaining it from your bookseller please contact Bookpoint Ltd, 39 Milton Park, Abingdon, Oxon OX14 4TD. Telephone: (44) 01235 400414, Fax: (44) 01235 400454. Lines are open from 9.00–6.00, Monday to Saturday, with a 24 hour message answering service. E-mail address: orders@bookpoint.co.uk

For U.S.A. & Canada order queries: please contact NTC/Contemporary Publishing, 4255 West Touhy Avenue, Lincolnwood, Illinois 60646–1975, U.S.A. Telephone: (847) 679 5500, Fax: (847) 679 2494.

Long renowned as the authoritative source for self-guided learning – with more than 30 million copies sold worldwide – the *Teach Yourself* series includes over 200 titles in the fields of languages, crafts, hobbies, business and education.

British Library Cataloguing in Publication Data
A catalogue entry for this title is available from The British Library.

Library of Congress Catalog Card Number: On file

First published in UK 2000 by Hodder Headline Plc, 338 Euston Road, London, NW1 3BH.

First published in US 2000 by NTC/Contemporary Publishing, 4255 West Touhy Avenue, Lincolnwood (Chicago), Illinois 60646–1975 U.S.A.

The 'Teach Yourself' name and logo are registered trade marks of Hodder & Stoughton Ltd.

Typeset by Transet Limited, Coventry, England.
Printed in Great Britain for Hodder & Stoughton Educational, a division of Hodder Headline Plc, 338 Euston Road, London NW1 3BH by Cox & Wyman Ltd, Reading, Berkshire.

Impression number   10 9 8 7 6 5 4 3 2
Year   2002 2001 2000

CONTENTS

READ THIS FIRST

If, like me, you usually skip introductions – don't turn the page. Read on! You need to know how *INSTANT* **Russian** works and why.

When I decided to write the *INSTANT* series I first called it *Barebones*, because that's what you want: *no frills, no fuss, just the bare bones and go!* So in *INSTANT* **Russian** you'll find:

- Fewer than 500 words – to say all, well … nearly all.
- No ghastly grammar – just a few useful tips.
- No time wasters such as … 'the pen of my aunt'.
- No phrase book phrases for vodka sampling sessions in Siberia.
- No need to struggle with the Russian script – everything is in easy phonetic language.
- No need to be perfect. Mistakes won't spoil your success.

I have put some 30 years of teaching experience into this course. I know how people learn. I also know for how long they are motivated by a new project (a few weeks) and how little time they can spare to study each day (under an hour). That's why you'll complete *INSTANT* **Russian** in six weeks and get away with 45 minutes a day.

Of course there is some learning to do, but I have tried to make it as much fun as possible, even the boring bits. You'll meet Tom and Kate Walker on holiday in Russia. They do the kinds of things you need to know about: shopping, eating out and getting about. As you will note, Tom and Kate speak *INSTANT* **Russian** all the time, even to each other. What paragons of virtue!

There are only two things you must do:

- Follow the Day-by-day guide as suggested. Please don't skip bits and short-change your success. Everything is there for a reason.
- Please buy the cassette that accompanies this book. It will also get you to speak faster and with confidence.

When you have filled in your Certificate at the end of the book and can speak *INSTANT* **Russian**, I would like to hear from you. You can write to me care of Hodder & Stoughton Educational.

Elizabeth Smith

HOW THIS
BOOK WORKS

INSTANT **Russian** has been structured for your rapid success.
This is how it works:

DAY-BY-DAY GUIDE Stick to it. If you miss a day, add one.

DIALOGUES Follow Tom and Kate through Russia. The English is in 'Russian-speak' to get you tuned in.

NEW WORDS Don't fight them, don't skip them – learn them! The flashcards will help you.

GOOD NEWS GRAMMAR After you read it you are allowed to forget half and still succeed! That's why it's Good News.

FLASH WORDS AND FLASH SENTENCES Read about these building blocks in the flashcard section on page 64. Then use them!

LEARN BY HEART Obligatory! Memorizing puts you on the fast track to speaking in full sentences.

LET'S SPEAK RUSSIAN *You* will be doing the talking – in Russian. Best with the tape.

SPOT THE KEYS Listen to rapid Russian and make sense of it.

SAY IT SIMPLY Learn how to use plain, *INSTANT* **Russian** to say what you want to say. Don't be shy!

TEST YOUR PROGRESS Mark your own test and be amazed by the result.

This is where you find the answers to the exercises.

This icon asks you to switch on the tape.

Pronunciation If you don't know it and don't have the tape, go straight to page 11. You need to know the pronunciation before you can start Week 1.

Progress Chart Enter your score each week and monitor your progress. Are you going for *very good* or *outstanding*?

Certificate It's on the last page. In six weeks it will have your name on it!

PROGRESS CHART

At the end of each week, record your test score on the progress chart below.

At the end of the course, throw out your worst result – everybody can have a bad week – and add up your *five* best weekly scores. Divide the total by five to get your average score and overall course result. Write your result – *outstanding*, *excellent*, *very good* or *good* – on your certificate.

If you scored more than 80%, enlarge it and frame it!

PROGRESS CHART

90–100%							*outstanding*
80–90%							*excellent*
70–80%							*very good*
60–70%							*good*
Weeks	1	2	3	4	5	6	

TOTAL OF FIVE BEST WEEKS _____

DIVIDED BY FIVE =

MY FINAL RESULT _____%

1 | WEEK ONE DAY-BY-DAY GUIDE

Study for 45 minutes – or a little longer if you can!

Day Zero
- Open the book and read READ THIS FIRST.
- Now read HOW THIS BOOK WORKS.

Day One
- Read IN THE AEROPLANE.
- Listen to/Read V SAMALYOTYE.
- Listen to/Read the NEW WORDS, then learn some of them.

Day Two
- Repeat V SAMALYOTYE and the NEW WORDS.
- Listen to/Read PRONUNCIATION.
- Learn more NEW WORDS.

Day Three
- Learn all the NEW WORDS until you know them well.
- Use the FLASH WORDS to help you.
- Read and learn GOOD NEWS GRAMMAR.

Day Four
- Cut out and learn the FLASH SENTENCES.
- Listen to/Read LEARN BY HEART.

Day Five
- Listen to/Read LET'S SPEAK RUSSIAN.
- Revise! Tomorrow you'll be testing your progress.

Day Six
- Translate TEST YOUR PROGRESS.

Day Seven
This is your day off!

Instant Russian

IN THE AEROPLANE

Tom and Kate Walker are on their way to Russia. They are boarding flight SU 254 to Yalta via Moscow and squeeze past Yuriy Zhivago who is sitting in their row.

Tom   Excuse me, please, by us (we have) seats 9a and 9b.

Yuriy   Yes? ... little minute (just a moment), please.

Tom   Hello. We – Tom and Kate Walker.

Yuriy   Hello. Me they call (I am called) Zhivago.

Tom   Dr Zhivago?

Yuriy   No, unfortunately. I – Yuriy Zhivago.

Tom   We are going to Yalta. You also?

Yuriy   No, I am going to Moscow. But I from Novgorod.

Tom   Novgorod very beautiful town. I was there in May, on business.

Yuriy   Who you? (What do you do?)

Tom   I programmer. Computers. I work at Unilever.

Yuriy   And you, Mrs Walker? Who you? Where do you work?

Kate   I worked in travel agency. Now I work in Rover. The work there better.

Yuriy   You from London?

Kate   No, we from Manchester. We were three years in London and a year in New York. Now we in Birmingham.

Yuriy   I worked in the university. Now I work in bank.

Kate   Work in bank good?

Yuriy   Work boring. But money (of money) more. By me (I have) big flat, Mercedes, wife, son and daughter. My wife from America. By her (she has) parents in Los Angeles and girlfriend in Florida. She always rings to them. It (is) costs expensive.

Kate   We now in holiday (on holiday). You also?

Yuriy   No, unfortunately. By me (I have) in August holiday. We are going to Greece. By us (we have) there house... summer home – without telephone.

🎵 📼 V SAMALYOTYE

Tom and Kate Walker are on their way to Russia. They are boarding flight SU 254 to Yalta via Moscow and squeeze past Yuriy Zhivago who is sitting in their row.

Tom   Eezveeneetye, pazhalusta, oo nas myesta 9a ee 9b.

Yuriy Da?... meenootachkoo, pazhalusta.

Tom   Zdravstvooeetye. Mi – Tom ee Kayeet Walker.

Yuriy Zdravstvooeetye. Myenya zavoot Zheevaga.

Tom   Doktar Zheevaga?

Yuriy Nyet, k sazhalyeniyu. Ya – Yuriy Zheevaga.

Tom   Mi yedyem v Yaltu. Vi tozhe?

Yuriy Nyet. Ya yedoo v Maskvoo. No ya eez Novgarada.

Tom   Novgorod ochyen kraseeviiy gorad. Ya tam bil v maye, pa beeznyesoo.

Yuriy Kto vi?

Tom   Ya pragrammeest. Kampyutyeri. Ya rabotayu v Ooneeleevyerye.

Yuriy A vi, meesees Walker? Kto vi? Gdye vi rabotayetye?

Kate   Ya rabotala v tooragyentstvye. Syeiychas ya rabotayu v Ro-oovyerye. Rabota tam loochshye.

Yuriy Vi eez Londana?

Kate   Nyet. Mi eez Manchyestyera. Mi bili tree goda v Londanye ee god v Nyu Yiyorke. Syeiychas mi v Beermeengkhamye.

Yuriy Ya rabotal v ooneevyerseetyetye. Syeiychas ya rabotayu v bankye.

Kate   Rabota v bankye kharoshaya?

Yuriy Rabota skoochnaya. No dyeneg bolshye. Oo myenya balshaya kvarteera, Mersyedyes, zhyena, sin ee doch. Maya zhyena eez Amyereekee. Oo nyeyo radeetyeli v Los Andzhyelyesye ee padrooga v Floreedye. Ana vsegda zvaneet eem. Eta stoeet doraga.

Kate   Mi syeiychas v otpooskye. Vi tozhe?

Yuriy Nyet, k sazhalyeniyu. Oo myenya v avgoostye otpoosk. Mi yedyem v Gryetseeyu. Oo nas tam dom... dacha – byez tyelyefona.

abcd... 📼 NEW WORDS

Learning words the traditional way can be boring. If you enjoy the
FLASHCARDS why not make your own for the rest of the words?
Always say the words ALOUD. It's the fast track to speaking!

v *in, to, at*
samalyot(ye) *aeroplane*
eezveeneetye *excuse me*
pazhalusta *please*
oo nas *by us (we have)*
myesta *places, seats*
a ... b *a... b* (pronounced *ah... bay*)
ee *and*
da *yes*
meenootachkoo *little minute*
zdravstvooeetye *hello*
mi *we*
myenya zavoot *they call me (I am called)*
nyet *no*
k sazhalyeniyu *unfortunately (towards regret)*
ya *I*
yedyem *we go (travel)*
yedoo *I go (travel)*
vi *you (polite)*
tozhye *also*
no *but*
eez *from*
ochyen *very*
kraseeviiy *beautiful*
gorad *town*
tam *there*
bil *was*
bilee *were*
v maye *in May*
dlya *for*
pa beeznyesoo *on business*
kto *who*

rabotayu *I work*
rabotayetye *you work*
pragrammeest *computer programmer*
kampyutyer/kampyutyeri *computer*
gdye *where*
rabotala *I, she worked*
rabotal *I, he worked*
v tooragyentstvye *in a/the travel agency*
syeiychas *now*
rabota *work, job*
loochshye *better*
tree *three*
goda/god *year*
v ooneevyerseetyetye *at a/the university*
bank / v bankye *bank/in, at bank*
kharoshaya *good*
skoochnaya *boring*
dyeneg *money*
bolshye *more*
oo myenya *I have*
balshaya *big*
kvarteera *flat*
maya, moiy *my*
zhyena *wife*
sin *son*
doch *daughter*
oo nyeyo *she has*
radeetyelee *parents*
padrooga *girlfriend*
ana *she*
vsyegda *always*

zvan**ee**t *rings, 'phones*
eem *to them*
eta *it is*
st**o**eet *costs*
d**o**raga *expensive*
v **o**tpooskye *on holiday*

v **a**vgoostye *in August*
tam *there*
dom *house*
d**a**cha *summer house*
byez tyelyef**o**na *without*
  telephone

TOTAL NEW WORDS: 74
...only 305 words to go!

Some easy extras

Myesyatsi (months)

yanvar, fyevral, mart, apr**ye**l, m**a**iy, ee**yu**n, ee**yu**l, **a**vgoost,
syent**ya**br, akt**ya**br, na**ya**br, d**ye**kabr

Tseefri (numerals)

adee**n** = 1
dva = 2
tree = 3
chyetirye = 4
p**ya**t = 5

shy**e**st = 6
syem = 7
v**o**syem = 8
d**ye**vyat = 9
d**ye**syat = 10

More greetings

d**o**braye **oo**tra *good morning*, d**o**briiy dyen *good day, good*
afternoon; d**o**briiy v**ye**chyer *good evening*; dasveed**a**neeya *good-bye*

🔊 PRONUNCIATION

The Russian language is beautiful, so drop all inhibitions and try to
speak Russian rather than English with the words changed. If the
Russian pronunciation is new to you please buy the cassette and
listen to the real thing.

As you can see all the words in *INSTANT* **Russian** have been
transliterated into phonetic language. That makes it much easier,
especially if you are in a hurry. You don't have to learn the Cyrillic
alphabet first but can start speaking straight away.

The guide to vowels and consonants will get you started. Sometimes
it takes a lot of English letters – for example *shsh* – to produce the
sound of one Russian letter, but you'll soon pick it up.

Vowels

Say the sound ALOUD and then the Russian example ALOUD.

a	*like* **a** *in father*	balshaya
e	*like* **e** *in let*	eta
ee	*like* **ee** *in feet*	eezveeneetye
i	*like* **i** *in ill*	mi
iy	*like* **y** *in boy*	kraseeviiy
o	*like* **o** *in bore*	Londan
oo	*like* **oo** *in shoot*	loochshye

y plus vowel

ya	*like* **ya** *in* **ya**rd	ya
ye	*like* **ye** *in* **ye**t	nyet
yo	*like* **yo** *in* **yo**nder	oo nyeyo
yu	*like* **u** *in* **u**niversal	ya rabotayu

Consonants

g	is always pronounced as a 'hard' g, as in *goat*	
r	is rolled (as in Italian)	
v	*like* **v** *in vase*, never like vee even when it's on its own	
zh	*like* **s** *in pleasure*	tozhe
kh	*like* **ch** *in loch*	kharoshaya
ts	*like* **ts** *in quits*	tsar
sh	*like* **sh** *in shout*	shyest
shsh	*like* **sh sh** *in posh ship*	yeshshyo
l', t'		rabotat', skol'ka

When you see a ' after a letter try to slip in a very soft y.

Accent

The letter in **bold** tells you to stress the syllable in which it appears. Example: Maskv**oo**, rab**o**tayu. The stress is especially important when you come across the vowel **o**. If it is stressed, it is pronounced like the **o** in *bore*; if it is not stressed, it is pronounced like the **a** in *sofa*.

When you go to Russia you'll want to know a little of the Cyrillic script, too. So, as an introduction here's the Russian alphabet. And later in the course there'll also be a few useful flash words in 'real' Russian script, to help you on your way.

А	Б	В	Г	Д	Е	Ё	Ж	З	И	Й	К	Л	М	Н	О	П	Р
а	б	в	г	д	е	ё	ж	з	и	й	к	л	м	н	о	п	р

С	Т	У	Ф	Х	Ц	Ч	Ш	Щ	Ъ	Ы	Ь	Э	Ю	Я
с	т	у	ф	х	ц	ч	ш	щ	ъ	ы	ь	э	ю	я

GOOD NEWS GRAMMAR

This is the Good News part of each week. Remember I promised *no ghastly grammar*! I simply explain the differences between Russian and English. This will help you to speak Russian *INSTANT*ly!

1 Words for 'the' and 'a'

There aren't any! So bank in Russian means either 'a bank' or 'the bank' and the plural bank**ee** means either 'some banks' or 'the banks'.

2 The Russian words for 'am', 'are', 'is'

There aren't any! So all you need to say in Russian is:

I computer programmer = Ya programme**ee**st

3 The Russian words for 'have', 'has'

There aren't any! Russian uses a different sort of phrase and says, literally, 'by me' (there is) = Oo men**ya**. Example: 'I have a flat' = Oo men**ya** kvart**ee**ra.

Here is the complete list. Spend ten minutes on it until you know it with your eyes closed.

oo men**ya**	*I have*
oo vas	*you have*
oo nyev**o**, oo nye**yo**	*he has, she has*
oo nas	*we have*
oo neekh	*they have*

4 Saying 'you'

Russian has two words for 'you'. If you know one person well, or are speaking to a child, use '*ti*'; if you are being polite and formal to one person use '*vi*' or if you are speaking to more than one person, also use '*vi*'. In *INSTANT Russian* you only use '*vi*'.

5 Doing things

Did you notice that when you say *I, we* or *you* in Russian the ending of the verb changes? Here are the verbs you came across in the dialogue. Have another look at them. They are not for learning. You have done that already.

rabotat' *to work*		yekhat' *to travel*	
ya rabotayu	*I work*	ya yedoo	*I travel*
mi rabotayem	*we work*	mi yedyem	*we travel*
vi rabotayetye	*you work*	vi yedyetye	*you travel*

6 'V' in, at, to

As you saw in the NEW WORDS the Russian letter v can mean in, at, to and sometimes even 'on', as in 'on holiday' – v otpooskye. That's the easy bit. Unfortunately, after a v the ending of the following word changes. So Yalta becomes Yaltu and bank becomes bankye. But don't worry about it. This is just for knowing, not for learning! You'll pick it up as you go along.

7 Asking questions

Vi tozhe. *You, too.* Vi tozhye? *You, too?* You simply use your voice to turn a statement into a question. Easy!

 LEARN BY HEART

Don't be tempted to skip this exercise because it reminds you of school… If you want to SPEAK, not stumble, saying a few lines by HEART does the trick!

Learn MYENYA ZAVOOT by heart after you have filled in the gaps with your personal, or any, information.

> Example: Myenya zavoot Colin Bell.
> Ya eez Londana.

When you know the seven lines by heart, go over them again until you can say them aloud fluently and fairly fast. Can you beat 40 seconds?

Myenya zavoot

Myenya zavoot ....(NAME)
Ya eez...(PLACE)
Ya rabotayu v bankye ....
Oo menya balshaya kvarteera. Ana doroga stoeet
V martye ya bil/bila v ....(PLACE)
V sentyabrye mi yedyem v..(PLACE)
Vi tozhye?

◯ ◁▭▷ LET'S SPEAK RUSSIAN

If you have the cassette, close the book and listen to LET'S SPEAK RUSSIAN. If you do not have the cassette, read on.

I'll give you ten English sentences and you put them into Russian. Always speak ALOUD. After each one check the answer at the bottom of this page. Tick each one that you get right.

1 I am called Tom Green.
2 Are you from London?
3 Yes, I am from London.
4 I have a girlfriend in Florida.
5 We are travelling to Moscow.
6 Do you have a Mercedes?
7 No, unfortunately not.
8 We have a house in Novgorod.
9 There is more money in the bank.
10 Is the job boring?

Well, how many did you tick? If you are not happy do it again.

Now here are some questions in Russian and you are going to answer in Russian. Answer the next five questions with '**da**' and '**ya**'.

11 Vi eez Manchyestyera?
12 Oo vas dom v Londanye?
13 Vi yedyetye v Maskvoo?
14 Vi rabotayete byez kompyutyera?
15 Vi bilee v Breestolye pa beeznyesoo?

And now answer the next five questions with '**da**' and '**mi**' or '**oo nas**'.

16 Vi yedyetye v Novgorod?
17 Oo vas myesta 9a ee 9b?
18 Oo vas otpoosk v apryelye?
19 Vi bilee tree goda v Londanye?
20 Oo vas syeiychas bolshye denyeg?

Answers to LET'S SPEAK RUSSIAN

1 Menya zavoot Tom Green.
2 Vi eez Londana?
3 Da, ya eez Londana.
4 Oo menya padrooga v Floreedye.
5 Mi yedyem v Maskvoo.
6 Oo vas Myersyedyes?
7 Nyet, k sazhalyeniyu.
8 Oo nas dom v Novgaradye.
9 V bankye bolshye dyenyeg.
10 Rabota skoochnaya?
11 Da, ya eez Manchyestyera.
12 Da, oo menya dom v Londanye.
13 Da, ya yedoo v Maskvoo.
14 Da, ya rabotayu byez kompyutyera.
15 Da, ya bil/bila v Breestolye pa beeznyesoo.
16 Da, mi yedyem v Novgorod.
17 Da, oo nas myesta 9a ee 9b.
18 Da, oo nas otpoosk v apryelye.
19 Da, mi bilee tree goda v Londanye.
20 Da, oo nas syeiychas bolshye denyeg.

Well, what was your score? If you ticked all of them give yourself three gold stars!

☑☒ TEST YOUR PROGRESS

This is your only **written** exercise. You'll be amazed at how easy it is! Translate the 20 sentences without looking at the previous pages. The bits in brackets help you with the difference between English and Russian.

(Please note: write the words straight: Don't alternate bold type and light to show where the word is stressed. It would take you forever!)

1 They call me (I am called) Frank Lukas.
2 Hello, we (are) Viktor and Olga.
3 I (am) also from Omsk.
4 In October I was in Moscow.
5 We were three years in America.
6 London is very expensive.
7 Excuse me, please. Where (do) you work?
8 Are you working in Manchester?
9 (Are) you Viktor Izmailov from Tomsk?
10 (The) flat in Novgorod is very big.
11 Little minute (just a moment), please, by me (I have) more money.
12 There there is (a) telephone? No, unfortunately not.
13 I (am) in Yalta without (my) son.
14 (Is) (the) company big?
15 (Is) (a) Mercedes expensive?
16 In April London (is) very beautiful.
17 By him (he has) in (the) travel agency (a) girlfriend.
18 Unfortunately (the) work (is) very boring.
19 (The) job is very good, but (a) holiday is better.
20 My daughter telephones always.

When you have finished look up the answers on page 60 and mark your work. Then enter your result on the Progress chart on page 6. If your score is higher than 80% you'll have done very well indeed!

2 | WEEK TWO
DAY-BY-DAY GUIDE

45 minutes a day – but a little extra will step up your progress!

Day One
- Read IN SAINT PETERSBURG.
- Listen to/Read V SANKT-PYETYERBOORGYE.
- Listen to/Read the NEW WORDS. Learn 20 easy ones.

Day Two
- Repeat V SANKT-PYETYERBOORGYE and NEW WORDS.
- Go over PRONUNCIATION.
- Learn the harder NEW WORDS.
- Use the FLASH WORDS to help you.

Day Three
- Learn all NEW WORDS until you know them well.
- Read and learn GOOD NEWS GRAMMAR.

Day Four
- Cut out and learn the FLASH SENTENCES.
- Listen to/Read LEARN BY HEART (page 24).

Day Five
- Listen to/Read LET'S SPEAK RUSSIAN.
- Go over LEARN BY HEART.

Day Six
- Translate TEST YOUR PROGRESS.

Day Seven
This is a study-free day!

🎧 IN SAINT PETERSBURG

In Saint Petersburg Tom and Kate are checking in at a hotel. They speak to Olga, the receptionist at the Service Desk and later to Ivan, the waiter.

Kate Good day. By you (do you have) room for two, for one night? Costs not too expensive?

Olga Yes, by us (we have) room with a bath and shower... but shower it is necessary to repair, it does not work.

Tom Where is room?

Olga On tenth floor.

Kate How much does it cost?

Olga Only 500 roubles per person, but credit cards we do not accept! Breakfast from 8 o'clock to 9.

Tom Well... we want room. But is it possible to have breakfast at 7.45? By us (we have) excursion tomorrow at 8.15.

Kate And I have question Where is it possible to drink coffee or tea? Where here café?

Olga Café from here is near, to the left, then to the right 30 metres, then straight on.

(In the café)

Ivan I am listening you (What can I get you?)

Kate For us coffee without sugar and tea with milk.

Ivan Is it all? By us (we have) sandwiches with cheese and with ham.

Tom One sandwich with cheese and one sandwich with ham, please.

Tom Cheese terrible.

Kate But ham good.

Tom Table too small.

Kate But toilets very clean

Tom My tea cold.

Kate But waiter very beautiful (handsome).

Tom Bill, please.

Ivan Fifty roubles.

▶ ■ V SANKT-PYETYERBOORGYE

In Saint Petersburg Tom and Kate are checking in at a hotel. They speak
to Olga, the receptionist at the Service Desk and later to Ivan, the waiter.

Kate   Dobriiy dyen. Oo vas yest nomyer na dvaeekh, na adnoo
noch? Stoeet nye sleeshkam doroga?

Olga   Da, oo nas nomyer s vannoiy ee s dooshyem … a doosh
nada atryemonteeravat', on nye rabotayet.

Tom   Gdye nomyer?

Olga   Na desyatam etazhye.

Kate   Skol'ka stoeet?

Olga   Tol'ka pyat'sot rooblyeiy na chyelovyeka, no kryedeetniye
kartachkee mi nye preeneemayem! Zavtrak s vasmee
chasov do dyevyatee.

Tom   Noo… mi khateem nomyer. A mozhna zavtrakat' v syem
sorak pyat? Oo nas ekskoorseeya zavtra v vosyem
pyatnadtsat.

Kate   Ee o myenya vapros. Gdye mozhna peet' kofye eelee chaiy?
Gdye zdyes kafe?

Olga   Kafe atsyuda bleezka, nalyeva, patom naprava treedtsat
myetrav, patom pryama.

(In the café)

Ivan   Slooshayu vas.

Kate   Nam kofye byez sakhara ee chaiy s malakom.

Ivan   Eta vsyo? Oo nas bootyerbrodi s siram ee s vyetchinoiy.

Tom   Adeen bootyerbrod s siram ee adeen bootyerbrod s
vyetcheenoiy, pazhalusta.

Tom   Sir oozhasniiy.

Kate   A vyetcheena kharoshaya.

Tom   Stol sleeshkam malyenkeeiy.

Kate   A tooalyeti ochyen cheestiye.

Tom   Moiy chaiy khalodniy.

Kate   A afeetseeant kraseeviiy.

Tom   Shyot, pazhalusta.

Ivan   Pyatdesyat rooblyeiy.

abcd... 🔲 **NEW WORDS**

dobriiy dyen *good day*

yest *there is /is there*

nomyer na dvaeekh *room for two* (i.e. *double room*)

na *for, on*

na adnoo noch *for one night*

nye *not*

sleeshkam *too* (as in *'too much'*)

s *with, from*

s vannoiy *with a bathroom*

doosh (s dooshyem) *shower (with a shower)*

a *and, but*

nada *it is necessary*

atryemonteeravat' *to repair*

on *it/he*

nye rabotayet *does not work*

na desyatam etazhye *on the tenth floor*

skol'ka *how much/how many*

tol'ka *only*

pyatsot *500*

rooblee, rooblyeiy *rouble(s)*

na chyelovyeka *for a person (per person)*

kryedeetniye kartachkee *credit cards*

preeneemayem *we accept*

zavtrak *breakfast*

s vasmee chasov *from eight hours (from 8 o'clock)*

do *until*

dyevyat/devyatee *nine*

noo... *well...*

mi khateem *we want*

mozhna *it is possible*

zavtrakat' *to have breakfast*

syem sorak pyat *7.45*

ekskoorseeya *excursion*

zavtra *tomorrow*

vosyem pyatnadtsat *8.15*

vapros *question*

kofye *coffee*

eelee *or*

chaiy *tea*

peet'/ya pyu *to drink/I drink*

zdyes *here*

kafe *café*

atsyuda *from here*

bleezka *close, near*

nalyeva *to the left, on the left*

naprava *to the right, on the right*

treedtsat myetrav *30 metres*

patom *then, next*

pryama *straight on*

slooshayu *I listen*

vi/vas *you*

nam *for us*

sakhar/sakhara *sugar*

malako/malakom *milk*

vsyo *all, everything*

bootyerbrod/ bootyerbrodi *sandwich/sandwiches*

sir/siram *cheese*

vyetchina/ vyetchinoiy *ham*

oozhasniiy *terrible*

stol *table*

malyenkiiy/malyenkaya *small*

tooalyeti *toilets*

cheestiye *clean*

khalodniy *cold*

afeetseeant *waiter*

shyot *bill*

pyatdesyat *50*

TOTAL NEW WORDS: 67
...only 238 words to go!

Some useful extras
Tseefri (numerals)

adeenadtsat = 11, dvyenadtsat = 12, treenadtsat = 13, chyetirnadtsat
= 14, pyatnadtsat = 15, shyestnadtsat = 16, syemnadtsat = 17,
vasyemnadtsat = 18, dyevyatnadtsat = 19, dvadtsat = 20,
treedtsat = 30, sorak = 40, pyatdyesyat = 50, shyestdyesyat
= 60, syemdyesyat = 70, vosyemdyesyat = 80, dyevyanosta = 90,
sto = 100, dvyestee = 200, treesta = 300, chyetiryesta = 400, pyatsot
= 500, shyestsot = 600, tisyacha = 1000 – You join numbers just
like in English: 23 = dvadtsat tree; 35 = treedtsat pyat.

Telling the time (vryemya)

chas *hour*, chasi *clock*, tree chasa *it is 3 o'clock*, v katoram chasoo?
at what time?, dva chasa *at 2 o'clock*, v tree chasa *at 3 o'clock*,
v pyat chasov *at 5 o'clock*, (v) syem treedtsat *(at) 7.30*,
meenoota *minute*, dyen *day*, nyedyelya *week*, myesyats *month*, god *year*

GOOD NEWS GRAMMAR

1 Doing things

In Week 1 you learned how to say **I, you, we**... work or travel.
Now let's complete the list with **he, she, it** and **they**... work or are working.

Barees rabotayet. On rabotayet.	Boris works. He is working.
Ol'ga rabotayet. Ana rabotayet.	Olga works. She is working.
Tyelyefon rabotayet. On rabotayet.	The telephone works. It is working.
Barees ee Ol'ga rabotayut.	Boris and Olga work.
Anee rabotayut.	They are working.

So it's '-yet' for one person and '-yut' for more. And if you want to use
the basic form, i.e. *to work* it's rabotat' (with an apostrophe at the end).

2 To want and to be able to/can

Here are two important verbs which you'll use all the time.
Unfortunately, they don't behave as well as rabotat'. I have put them
into gift boxes for you so you won't forget. Spend five minutes on each.

Use *want* instead of *would like*. It does not sound at all rude in Russian.

WANT khatyet'		CAN moch'	
ya khachoo	*I want*	ya magoo	*I can*
vi khateetye	*you want*	vi mozhyete	*you can*
mi khateem	*we want*	mi mozhyem	*we can*
on, ana,		on, ana,	
ano khochyet	*he, she, it wants*	ano mozhyet	*he, she, it can*
anee khatyat	*they want*	anee mogoot	*they can*

3 Nada: the necessary and mozhna: the possible

These are two very useful words. Remember when Olga said that the shower needed repairing:

Nada atryemanteeravat'...   It is necessary to repair...

And then Tom wondered if they could have breakfast earlier:

Mozhna zavtrakat'?   Is it possible to have breakfast?

When you use nada and mozhna you'll carry on with the basic verb – just like in English. It is necessary/possible *to* work/eat: nada/mozhna rabotat'/peet', etc.

4 Word order: very relaxed!

'We don't accept credit cards' could be either:

        kryedeetniye kartochkee mi nye preeneemayem.

or   mi nye preeneemayem kryedeetniye kartachkee.

Take your pick!

5 Nyet and nye

Everyone knows 'nyet' – no?

Its 'brother' nye (not) is used when you are *not* doing something.

I don't work: ya nye rabotayu.

He's not working: on ne rabotayet.

6 ... and now for the Bad News: Endings

There are three types of nouns in Russian: masculine, feminine and neuter. You can often identify which is which by the ending – usually a *consonant* (masculine), an *a* (feminine) or an *o* (neuter). The trouble starts when you use a noun in a sentence. Take sir: cheese. Take *bread with cheese*: bootyerbrod s siram. Sir changes to siram. Adjectives and numbers behave equally badly: *new* could be: noviy, novim, novaya ... and more! But don't despair. You'll pick them up as you go along. Mistakes are allowed and won't cramp your style.

⬤ ▭ LET'S SPEAK RUSSIAN

Now let's practise what you have learned. I'll give you ten English sentences and you say them in Russian – ALOUD! If you don't have the cassette, cover up the answers. Tick each sentence if you got it right. Unless you got all ten correct, do the exercise again.

1 We would like a double room.
2 Unfortunately, it is too expensive.
3 Breakfast is at what time?
4 The telephone does not work.
5 We want sandwiches.
6 Do you also have tea?
7 Where is the café, left or right?
8 The toilets are not clean.
9 Can I please have the bill?
10 Tomorrow I am in London at 9 o'clock.

Now answer in Russian. Use '**da**' and '**mi**' for the ones on the left and '**nyet**' and '**ya**' for the ones on the right.

11 Oo vas yest kredeetnaya kartachka?

14 Vi khateetye yest' v vosyem chasov?

12 Vi khateetye yekhat' v Maskvoo?

15 Vi mozhyete rabotat' zavtra?

13 Oo vas zdyes tyelyefon?

16 Vi khateetye nomyer?

Now answer the last two using the words in brackets.

17 Gdye zdyes kafe? (bleezka, atsyuda)
18 V katoram chasoo vi khateetye yest'? (shyest sorak pyat)

ANSWERS TO LET'S SPEAK RUSSIAN

1 Mi khateem nomyer na dvaeekh.
2 K sazhalyeniyu eta stoeet sleeshkam doraga.
3 Zavtrak v katoram chasoo?
4 Tyelyefon nye rabotayet.
5 Mi khateem bootyerbrodi.
6 Oo vas chaiy tozhye?
7 Gdye kafe, nalyeva eelee naprava?
8 Tooalyeti ne cheestiye.
9 Shyot, pazhalusta.

10 Zavtra ya v Londanye v dyevyat chasov.
11 Da, oo nas yest kryedeetnaya kartochka.
12 Da, mi khateem yekhat' v Maskvoo.
13 Da, oo nas zdyes (yest') tyelyefon.
14 Nyet, ya nye khachoo yest' v vosyem chasov.
15 Nyet, ya nye magoo rabotat' zavtra.
16 Nyet, ya nye khachoo nomyer.
17 Kafe bleezka atsyuda.
18 Ya khachoo yest' v shyest sorak pyat.

Instant **Russian**

♥ 📼 *LEARN BY HEART*

Choose one of these to fill in the gaps: ma**ee**m m**oo**zhyem (husband), ma**yeiy** zhyen**oiy** (wife), ma**ee**m dr**oo**gam (friend), ma**yeiy** padr**oo**goiy (girlfriend). Try to say it in 45–60 seconds.

Oo menya mala dyenyeg, no...

Oo menya ma**la*** d**ye**nyeg, no ya khach**oo** **o**tpoosk v m**a**ye.

Ya khach**oo** **ye**khat' v Sankt-Pyetyerb**oo**rg s...

Ya khach**oo** v Sankt-Pyetyerb**oo**rgye peet' mn**o**ga** shamp**an**skava ee yest' b**oo**terbr**o**di. **E**ta vazm**o**zhna***? Da, eta ny**e**doraga st**o**eet. Tol'ka pyat's**o**t roobl**yeiy** na chyelov**ye**ka, ee oo menya kryed**ee**tnaya k**a**rtachka...

---

*mala: *a little*   **mnoga: *a lot, many*   ***vazmozhna: *it is possible*

☑☒ *TEST YOUR PROGRESS*

Translate these sentences into Russian and write them out. See what you can remember without looking at the previous pages. (Remember. Don't highlight the part of the word which is stressed.)

1 I drink a lot of champagne.
2 How much is (costs) breakfast, please?
3 Is there a travel agency here?
4 Do you have a table? At 7.15?
5 I would like to drink (some) coffee.
6 My holiday in Florida was better.
7 Where is there a good hotel?
8 Can I have the telephone bill, please?
9 We were in Saint Petersburg in May.
10 My house is too big.
11 At what time are you in Moscow tomorrow?
12 I am there from eight until five.
13 Excuse me, please. Where are the toilets, straight ahead?
14 We want to travel to Oslo in January, but it is too cold.
15 Does that cost more money?
16 Tomorrow where are you at 10.30?
17 It's terrible. The (hotel) room is very expensive.
18 Is it possible to drink coffee here now? Do you have seats?
19 We have a small house in America, but it is very expensive.
20 Goodbye, we are going to Yalta.

Check your answers with the key on page 61 and work out your score. Now enter your result on the Progress chart in the front of the book. If it is above 70% you have done very well.

3 | WEEK THREE
DAY-BY-DAY GUIDE

Study for 45 minutes a day – but there are no penalties for more!

Day One
- Read WE GO SHOPPING.
- Listen to/Read MI **DYE**LAYEM PAKOOPKEE.
- Listen to/Read NEW WORDS, then learn some of them.

Day Two
- Repeat MI **DYE**LAYEM PAKOOPKEE and NEW WORDS.
- Learn all the NEW WORDS. Use the FLASHCARDS!

Day Three
- Test yourself on all NEW WORDS.
  Boring, boring, but you are over halfway already!
- Read and learn GOOD NEWS GRAMMAR (page 30).
- Go over GOOD NEWS GRAMMAR.

Day Four
- Listen to/Read LEARN BY HEART (page 32).
- Cut out and learn the ten FLASH SENTENCES.

Day Five
- Listen to/Read SPOT THE KEYS (page 29).
- Listen to/Read LET'S SPEAK RUSSIAN (page 31).

Day Six
- Go over LEARN BY HEART.
- Have a quick look at NEW WORDS Weeks 1–3.
- You know over 200 words by now! Well, more or less.
- Translate TEST YOUR PROGRESS.

Day Seven
Enjoy your day off!

🔊 LET'S GO SHOPPING

Tom and Kate are staying in Moscow. Kate is planning some shopping.

Kate Well, today for us it is necessary to do shopping. First we go to centre of town on bus.

Tom But weather bad. (It is) Cold. And on television much sport. At 12.30 goes (is on) golf...

Kate Sorry, but for us it is necessary (to go) to bank, to post office for stamps, then to chemists, to dry cleaners and to supermarket.

Tom Well, golf not possible to watch... perhaps football at 3 o'clock. Is that all?

Kate No, for us it is necessary also to department store for new suitcase and to hairdresser's. And I want also (to go) to jewellery shop and to shop of souvenirs.

Tom Good grief! Shops open until what time?

Kate Until 6.30, it seems.

Tom Ah, football also not possible to watch... perhaps tennis at 8.30...

(Later)

Kate It seems, I too many presents bought. Bottle of champagne, tin of caviar, Russian dolls, chocolate.

Tom No problem! For us it is necessary to buy many presents. But what there, in big bag? Is it for me?

Kate And yes and no. I was in a jewellery shop, then in department store. In jewellery shop I saw brooch. It is amber brooch. Splendid, isn't it true? Shop assistant was very pleasant and so handsome as Tom Cruise.

Tom Who such (who is) Tom Cruise? And how much costs brooch?

Kate A little expensive... 600 roubles.

Tom What?... Crazy!

Kate But here is T-shirt. It not very expensive costs. And here's English newspaper... and on television now is going (is on) tennis, isn't it true?

⚆ ▣ *MI DYELAYEM PAKOOPKEE*

Tom and Kate are staying in Moscow. Kate is planning some shopping.

Kate   Noo, syevodnya nam nada dyelat' pakoopkee. Snachala mi yedyem v tsentr gorada na avtoboosye.

Tom   No pagoda plakhaya. Kholadna. Ee po tyelyeveezaroo mnoga sporta. V dvyenadtsat treedtsat eedyot golf...

Kate   Ezveenee, no nam nada v bank, na pochtoo za markamee, patom v aptyekoo, v kheemcheestkoo ee v soopyermarkyet.

Tom   Noo, golf nyelzya smatryet'... mozhyet bit' footbol v tree chasa. Eta vsyo?

Kate   Nyet, nam nada tozhye v oonivyermag za novim chyemodanom ee v pareekhmakhyerskooyu. Ee ya khachoo tozhye v yuvyeleerniy magazeen ee v magazeen soovyeneerav.

Tom   Bozhye moiy! Magazeeni atkriti do kakova chasa?

Kate   Do shyestee eelee do vasmee, kazhetsa.

Tom   Akh, footbol tozhye nyelzya smatryet'... mozhyet bit' tyennees v vosyem treedtsat...

(Later)

Kate   Kazhetsa, ya sleeshkam mnoga podarkav koopeela. Bootilkoo shampanskava, bankoo eekri, matryoshkee, shakalad.

Tom   Nyet prablyem! Nam nada koopeet' mnoga padarkav. A shto tam v balshoiy soomkye? Eta dlya menya?

Kate   Ee da ee nyet. Ya bila v yuvyeleernam magazeenye, patom v oonivyermagye. V yuvyeleernam magazeenye ya ooveedyela broshkoo. Eta yantarnaya broshka. Pryekrasnaya, ne pravda lee? Pradavyets bil ochyen preeyatniiy ee takoiy zhye krasavyets, kak Tom Cruise.

Tom   Kto takoiy Tom Cruise? Ee skol'ka stoeet broshka?

Kate   Nyemnozhka doraga. Shyestsot (600) rooblyeiy.

Tom   Shto? S ooma sashla!

Kate   No vot footbolka. Stoeet nye ochyen doraga. A vot angleeskaya gazyeta... a po tyelyeveezaroo syeiychas eedyot tyennees, nye pravda lee?

abcd... ▣ NEW WORDS

Learn the NEW WORDS in half the time using flash cards. There are 18 to start you off. Get a friend to make the rest!

syev**o**dnya *today*
d**y**elat' *to do*
pak**oo**pkee *the shopping*
snach**a**la *first*
tsentr *centre*
avt**o**boos *bus*
pag**o**da *weather*
plakh**a**ya *bad*
kh**o**ladna *cold*
po *on, along, according to*
tyelyev**ee**zar/tyelyev**ee**zaroo *television*
sp**o**rt/sp**o**rta/sp**o**rtoo *sport*
eed**yo**t *(he, she) it goes, is going*
ezveenee *I am sorry* (informal)
p**o**chta/p**o**chtoo *post office*
za *for, behind, beyond*
m**a**rkee/m**a**rkamee *stamps*
apt**ye**ka/apt**ye**koo *chemist's shop*
kheemch**ee**stka/kheemch**ee**stkoo *dry cleaner's*
soopyerm**a**rkyet *supermarket*
nyelz**ya** *it is not possible, one may not*
smatr**ye**t' *to watch*
m**o**zhyet bit' *perhaps*
v tree chasa *at 3 o'clock*
oonivyerm**a**g *department store*
n**o**viy/n**o**vim *new*
chyemod**a**n/chyemod**a**nom *suitcase*
pareekhm**a**khyerskaya/pareekh-m**a**khyerskooyu *hairdresser*
yuvyel**ee**erniy *jewellery* (adj)

magaz**ee**n/magaz**ee**ni *shop/shops*
soovyen**ee**ri/soovyen**ee**rav *souvenirs*
B**o**zhye moiy! *Good grief!* (lit: *God my!*)
atkr**i**ti *open* (plural form)
do kak**o**va chas**a**? *until when?*
k**a**zhetsa *it seems, I think/believe*
t**ye**nnees *tennis*
mn**o**ga *many*
koop**ee**la *(I) bought*
boot**i**lkoo shamp**a**nskava *bottle (of) Champagne*
pad**a**rkee/pad**a**rkav *presents*
b**a**nka/b**a**nkoo *tin, jar*
eekr**a**/eekr**i** *caviar*
matr**yo**shka/matr**yo**shkee *Russian doll/dolls* (fit one inside other)
shakal**a**d *chocolate*
nyet prabl**ye**m! *no problem!*
koop**ee**t' *to buy*
shto *what, that*
s**oo**mka, s**oo**mkye/pak**ye**teek *bag*
dlya men**ya** *for me*
oov**ee**dyet'/oov**ee**dyela *to see/she saw*
br**o**shka/br**o**shkoo *brooch*
yant**a**rnaya *amber*
pryekr**a**snaya *splendid*
ne pr**a**vda lee *isn't it?*
pradav**ye**ts *shop assistant*
pree**ya**tniiy *pleasant*
tak**oi**y zhye... kak *just as... as*

krasavyets   *handsome fellow*
kto tak**oiy**… ?   *Who is… ?*
nyemn**o**zhka   *a little*
s ooma sashla   *crazy!* (to a
   man one would say: s ooma
   sash**yol**)

vot   *here (there) is/are*
footb**o**lka   *T-shirt*
angl**ee**skaya/Angleeya,
   Anglee-ee   *English/England*
gaz**y**eta   *newspaper*

**TOTAL NEW WORDS: 65
...only 173 words to go!**

More extras

Tsvyeta (colours)

b**ye**liy	*white*	zyel**yo**niy	*green*
ch**yo**rniy	*black*	ar**a**nzhyeviy	*orange*
kr**a**sniy	*red*	r**o**zaviy	*pink*
seeneey	*blue*	s**ye**riy	*grey*
zh**yo**ltiy	*yellow*	kar**ee**chnyeviy	*brown*

SPOT THE KEYS

By now you can say many things in Russian. But what happens if you ask a question and don't understand the answer – hitting you at the speed of an automatic rifle? The smart way is not to panic, but to listen out for the words you know. Any familiar words which you pick up will provide you with key words – clues to what the other person is saying.

If you have the cassette listen to the dialogue. If you don't – read on. You are trying to ask the way to the post office…

YOU   Eezveen**ee**tye, pazh**a**lusta, gdye p**o**chta?
ANSWER   *Noo, eta ne tak prosta. Snachala eedeetye* pryama do *slyedooyushchyevaperekryostka, tamgdyenakhodeetsa* balshoiy   krasniy   dom.   Patom   nalyeva, *vi   ooveedeetye   tam   yeshshyo* magazeeni. *Yeshshyopadalshye   eedeetye   naprava. Vi ooveedeetye* aptyekoo *naproteev* pochti.

Did you hear the key words? pr**ya**ma do – balsh**oiy** kr**a**sniy dom – pat**om** – nal**ye**va – magaz**ee**ni – apt**ye**koo – p**o**chti.

I think you'll get there!

🔊 GOOD NEWS GRAMMAR

1 The past

This is easier than in French! Here's a very basic 'recipe':

- Take the basic form of the verb, say, rab**o**tat'.
- Take off the 't' and add an 'L' if you are talking about ONE MALE person (it could be Boris or yourself): Bar**ee**s rab**o**tal.
- Add 'LA' for ONE FEMALE person (it could be Tanya or you): T**a**nya rab**o**tala.
- Add 'LO' for neuter nouns: rad**ee**a ne rabotalo (pronounced rabotala).
- Add 'LEE' for you ('vi') and everything that's more than ONE: Boris and Tanya, we, they … rab**o**talee.

Most important: learn all the sample phrases which are in the past.

2 Nada, mozhna *and* nyelzya

Remember n**a**da and m**o**zhna from Week 2? It is necessary. It is possible. Here's another one: nyelz**ya**: it's not possible.

These three are very useful when you want to say can, can't or must, because that's really what they express: I can... for me it's possible. I can't … for me it's not possible. I must … for me it's necessary.

So all you need to do now is to add: *for me, for you, for us* etc. Here's the full list using *n**a**da* and *must buy* as an example:

mnye nada koop**ee**t'	*for me it is necessary... I must buy*
vam nada koop**ee**t'	*for you it is necessary… you must* buy
nam nada koop**ee**t'	*for us it is necessary... we must buy*
yem**oo**/y**ei**y nada koop**ee**t'	*for him/her it is necessary...* *he/she must buy*
eem nada koop**ee**t'	*for them it is necessary...* *they must buy.*

So now you can mix and match. Mnye m**o**zhna koop**ee**t': I can buy. Nam nyelz**ya** rab**o**tat': We can't work.

3 To go: eedtee' *on foot and* yekhat' *by transport*

Here's another gift box to help you remember these two:

ya eed**oo**	I go	ya y**e**doo
vi eedy**o**tye	you go	vi y**e**dyetye
on, an**a** eedy**o**t	he, she goes	on, an**a** y**e**doot
mi eed**yo**m	we go	mi **yed**yem
an**ee** eed**oo**t	they go	an**ee** y**e**doot

◑ ▭ LET'S SPEAK RUSSIAN

Over to you! If you have the cassette, close the book now. If you don't, cover up the answers below. Always answer ALOUD! Start with a ten-point warm-up. Say in Russian:

1 Now I am going to (the) post office.
2 Until what time (are the) shops open?
3 I am sorry, but that is too expensive.
4 From where bus goes to centre?
5 We bought souvenirs in Novgorod.
6 Can one buy caviar in the supermarket?
7 Shopping without money? No, but I have credit card.
8 I everything bought in the department store.
9 We must watch the weather on television
10 Good grief! The television doesn't work!

Answer the following using the words in brackets.

11 Oo vas yest' **s**eeneeye footb**o**lkee? (da, oo nas)
12 Vi koop**ee**lee m**a**rkee v soopyerm**a**rkyetye? (da, mi)
13 Vi rab**o**talee v b**a**nkye? (nyet, mi)
14 Vam n**a**da eedt**ee** v d**y**evyat chas**o**v? (nyet, nam)
15 Oo vas mn**o**ga d**y**enyeg? (nyet, oo nas)
16 Shto vi koop**ee**lee? Shakal**a**d **ee**lee shamp**a**nskaye? (shakal**a**d)
17 Kto smatr**y**el footb**o**l po tyelyev**ee**zaroo? (ya)
18 Do kak**o**va chas**a** magaz**ee**nee atkr**i**ti? (vasm**ee** chas**o**v)
19 Vi khat**ee**tye dv**y**estee pyatdes**ya**t gram (250 gr) **ee**lee pyats**o**t gram k**o**fye? (pyats**o**t gram).
20 Avt**o**boos **y**edyet v tsentr? (da)

Answers to LET'S SPEAK RUSSIAN

1 Seiych**a**s ya eed**oo** na p**o**chtoo.
2 Magaz**ee**ni atkr**i**ti do kak**o**va chas**a**?
3 Ezv**ee**nee, no **e**ta sl**ee**shkam d**o**raga.
4 Atk**oo**da atv**o**boos **y**edyet v tsentr?
5 Mi koop**ee**lee soovyen**ee**ree v N**o**vgaradye.
6 M**o**zhna koop**ee**t' **ee**kro v soopyerm**a**rkyete?
7 Dyel**a**t' pak**oo**pkee byez d**y**enyeg? Nyet, no oo my**e**nya kryed**ee**tnaya k**a**rtachka.
8 Ya vsyo koop**ee**la v soopyerv**y**erm**a**gye.
9 Nam n**a**da smatr**y**et' pag**o**doo po tyelyev**ee**zaroo.
10 B**o**zhye moiy! Tyelyev**ee**zar nye rab**o**tayet!

11 Da, oo nas yest' **s**eeneeye footb**o**lkee.
12 Da, mi koop**ee**lee m**a**rkee v soopyerm**a**rkyetye.
13 Nyet, mi nye rab**o**talee v b**a**nkye.
14 Nyet, nam nye n**a**da eedt**ee** v d**y**evyat' chas**o**v.
15 Nyet, oo nas m**a**la d**y**enyeg.
16 Mi koop**ee**lee (ya koop**ee**l/ya koop**ee**la) shakal**a**d.
17 Ya smatr**y**ela footb**o**l po tyelyev**ee**zaroo.
18 Do vasm**ee** (chas**o**v).
19 Mi khat**ee**m (ya khach**oo**) pyats**o**t gram.
20 Da, avt**o**boos **y**edyet v tsentr.

Instant Russian

♥ 📼 LEARN BY HEART

Say these seven lines in under 50 seconds. The more expression you use the easier it will be to remember all the useful bits.

> Syevodnya nam nada dyelat' pakoopkee – nyet prablyem!
> No atkooda* yedyet avtoboos v magazeeni?
> Akh, bozhye moiy! Kazhetsa, oo menya mala dyenyeg.
> Mi koopeelee mnoga padarkav: matryoshkee, broshkoo ee bankoo eekree.
> Eta bila doroga: shyestsot roobleiy, no pradavyets bil ochyen preeyatniy.

*atkooda: *from where*

☑☒ TEST YOUR PROGRESS

Translate these sentences into Russian. Then check your answers and be amazed!

1 Where is (the) sales assistant?
2 Where is it possible to buy sandwiches?
3 When must you (go) to England today? At 7 o'clock?
4 We saw that yesterday on television.
5 Now (the) shops (are) open, it seems.
6 Here there is (a) department store or (a) centre with shops?
7 Excuse me, are you also going to the post office?
8 Where did you buy (the) English newspaper?
9 Do you want coffee or tea?
10 The weather is bad today. It is not possible to go to Novgorod.
11 That is all? That was not expensive.
12 The stamps cost 15 roubles.
13 We accept credit cards.
14 Is 300 grams cheese too much? No, no problem.
15 There is (a) new dry cleaner's near here.
16 Do you have (a) bag for my T-shirt, please?
17 I saw here (a) chemist's, it seems.
18 Good grief! (The) bus has broken down (isn't working) and (the) Mercedes also has broken down (isn't working)!
19 Did you see (the) T-shirt? Where did you buy it?
20 Five hundred roubles, but I have only dollars.

4 | WEEK FOUR
DAY-BY-DAY GUIDE

Study 35 minutes a day but if you are keen try 40… 45…!

Day One
- Read WE ARE GOING TO THE RESTAURANT.
- Listen to/Read MI EEDYOM V RYESTORAN.
- Listen to/Read the NEW WORDS. Learn the easy ones.

Day Two
- Repeat the dialogue. Learn the harder NEW WORDS.
- Cut out the FLASH WORDS to help you.

Day Three
- Learn all the NEW WORDS until you know them well.
- Read and learn the GOOD NEWS GRAMMAR.

Day Four
- Listen to/Read LEARN BY HEART.
- Cut out and learn the ten FLASH SENTENCES.

Day Five
- Listen to/Read SPOT THE KEYS.
- Read SAY IT SIMPLY.

Day Six
- Listen to/Read LET'S SPEAK RUSSIAN.
- Translate TEST YOUR PROGRESS.

Day Seven
Are you keeping your scores over 60%? In that case …
Have a good day off!

❻ WE ARE GOING TO (THE) RESTAURANT

Tom and Kate are still in Moscow. Boris Vadimovich is inviting them to dinner.

Kate   Tom, someone rang. He did not say why. The number is on paper, by telephone. Some Boris...

Tom   Oh, yes, Boris Vadimovich, good customer of our firm. I him well know. Very pleasant person. By me meeting with him on Thursday. Very important matter.

Tom   *(On the phone)* Hello, good morning, Boris Vadimovich... Speaks Tom Walker... Yes, thank you... yes, of course, it is possible... next week... of course... yes... very interesting... no, by us time there is... splendid... no, only for a few days... I understand... when?... at 8 o'clock... upstairs by exit, by door. Well, until Tuesday, thank you very much, good-bye.

Kate   What are we doing on Tuesday?

Tom   We are going to restaurant with Boris Vadimovich. Restaurant in centre behind church. He says, that restaurant new. Boris Vadimovich in Moscow for two days, with Edith and Peter Palmer from our firm.

Kate   I know Edith Palmer. She is boring and knows everything. She has a terrible dog. I think, that on Tuesday I will be ill. Heavy cold and everything hurts. The doctor necessary it will be to call...

Tom   Please, thus it is not possible (one can't do that). Mr Vadimovich is very important client.

In the restaurant:

Waiter   Here's the menu. Today by us also firm's dishes (specials) – fish, and for sweet course – walnut cake.

Boris   What for you, Mrs Walker? Soup you want? Meat or fish?

Kate   For me steak with salad, please.

Edith   To eat much red meat is harmful, Kate.

Boris   Mr Walker, what for you? And what you want to drink? Wine?

Tom   Beer, then sausage with fried potato, please.

┅➡ Page 36

⬤⬤ 📼 MI EEDYOM V RYESTORAN

Tom and Kate are still in Moscow. Boris Vadimovich is inviting them to dinner.

Kate Tom, kto-ta pazvaneel. On nye skazal, pachemoo. Nomyer na boomagye, okala tyelyefona. Kakoiy-ta Barees.

Tom Akh, da, Barees Vadeemaveech, kharosheeiy kleeyent nasheiy feermi. Ya yevo kharasho znayu. Ochyen preeyatniy chyelavyek. Oo menya sveedaneeye s neem v chyetvyerg. Ochyen vazhnaye dyela.

Tom *(on the phone)* Alo, dobraye ootra, Barees Vadeemaveech. Gavareet Tom Walker... Da, spaseeba... da, kanyeshna vazmozhna... na slyedooyushshyeiy nyedyele... kanyeshna... da... ochyen eentyeryesna... nyet, oo nas vryemya yest... pryekrasna... nyet, tol'ka na nyeskal'ka dnyeiy... Ya panimayu... kagda?... v vosyem chasov... navyerkhoo, okala vikhada, okala dvyeree. Noo, do vtorneeka, spaseeba balshoiy, dasveedaniya.

Kate Shto mi dyelayem va vtorneek?

Tom Mi eedyom v ryestoran s Bareesam Vadeemaveech. Ryestoran v tsentrye, za tserkvyu. On gavareet, shto ryestoran noviy. Barees Vadeemaveech v Maskvye na dva dnya, s Edith i Peeterom Palmyer eez nasheiy feermi.

Kate Ya znayu Edith Palmyer. Ana skoochnaya ee vsyo znayet loochshye vsyekh. Oo nyeyo oozhasnaya sabaka. Ya doomayu, shto va vtorneek ya boodoo bal'na. Prastooda ee vsyo baleet. Vracha nada boodyet vizvat'...

Tom Pazhalusta, tak nyelzya, tak ne gadeetsa. Barees Vadeemaveech ochyen vazhniiy kleeyent.

In the restaurant:

Waiter Vot myenyu. Syevodnya oo nas tozhye feermyeniye blyuda – riba, ee na sladkaye – aryekhaviy tort.

Boris Shto vam, gaspazha Walker? Soop khateetye? Myasa eelee riboo?

Kate Mnye beefshteks s salatam, pazhalusta.

Edith Yest' mnoga tyomnava myasa vryedna, Kate.

Boris Gaspadeen Walker, shto vam? Ee shto vi khateetye peet'? Veeno?

Tom Peeva, patom kalbasoo s zharyennaiy kartoshkaiy, pazhalusta.

⸺➤ Page 37

Edith But Tom, that's very greasy! I would not want to eat such dishes.

Boris And you, Mrs Palmer?

Edith Small piece of chicken from grill, fruit and glass of water.

(Later)

Boris Everyone ready? It is already late. Who wants coffee? No one? Good, bill, please.

Edith Oh, Boris Vadimovich, you can me help, please? How in Russian 'doggy bag'? I want bag for my dog.

Kate But Edith, your dog in England!

abcd... **NEW WORDS**

kto-ta *someone*
pazvaneet'/pazvaneel *to ring/he rang*
on/yevo/neem *he, him*
skazat'/skazal *to say/he said*
pachemoo *why*
nomyer *number*
boomaga/boomagye *paper*
okala *near, by*
kakoiy-ta *some (sort of)*
kleeyent *customer*
kharasho *good, well*
feerma/feermi *firm*
znat'/znayu/znayet *to know/ I know/he/(she) knows*
chyelavyek *person*
sveedaneeye *meeting*
chyetvyerg *Thursday*
vazhnaye *important*
dyela *matter*
gavareet'/gavareet *to speak, to say/he speaks, he says*
spaseeba/balshoiy *thank you/very much*
kanyeshna *of course*
vazmozhna *it is possible*
slyedooyushshyeiy *next*
eentyeryesna *it is interesting*

vryemya *time*
nyeskal'ka *a few*
dnyeiy/dnya *days*
kakda *when*
navyerkhoo *upstairs*
vikhad/vikhada *exit*
dvyer/dvyeree *door*
vtorneek/vtorneeka *Tuesday*
tserkav/tserkvyu *church*
skoochnaya *boring*
oozhasnaya *terrible*
sabaka *dog*
doomat'/doomayu *to think/ I think*
boodoo/boodyet *I will be/he (she, it) will be*
bal'na *ill, sick*
prastooda *cold*
baleet *it hurts*
vrach/vracha *doctor*
vizvat'... *to summon, call, send for*
tak *thus, so*
ne gadeetsa *it does not fit (it's not on)*
myenyu *menu*
feermyeniye blyuda *firm's dishes (i.e. specials)*
riba/riboo *fish*

Edith   No Tom, eta ochyen zheerna! Ya ne khatyela bi yest' takoye blyuda.

Boris   A vi, gaspazha Palmyer?

Edith   Malyenkiy koosochyek kooreetsi, s greelya, frookti ee stakan vadi.

(Later)

Boris   Vsye gatovi? Oozhye pozdna. Kto khochyet kofye? Neekto? Kharasho, shyot, pazhalusta.

Edith   Akh, Barees Vadeemaveech, vi nye mozhyete mnye pamoch', pazhalusta? Kak pa-rooskee 'doggy bag'? Ya khachoo pakyeteek dlya moyeiy sabakee.

Kate   No Edith, vasha sabaka v Anglee-ee!

sladkaye	*sweet, dessert*	zheerna	*it is greasy*
aryekhaviy tort	*walnut cake*	koosochyek	*piece*
gaspazha	*Mrs*	kooreetsa/kooreetsi	*chicken*
soop	*soup*	greel'/greelya	*grill*
myasa	*meat*	frookt	*fruit*
beefshteks	*steak*	stakan	*glass*
salat/salatam	*salad*	vada/vadi	*water*
tyomnava myasa	*dark (red) meat*	gatovi	*ready*
vryedna	*it is harmful*	oozhye	*already*
gaspadeen	*Mr*	pozdna	*it is late*
veeno	*wine*	neekto	*no one*
peeva	*beer*	pamoch'	*to help*
kalbasa/kalbasoo	*sausage*	kak pa-rooskee	*how in*
zharyenaiy kartoshkaiy	*fried*		*Russian*
potato			

> **TOTAL NEW WORDS: 75**
> **... only 98 words to go!**

Last extras

Days of the week

panyedyel'neek	*Monday*	pyatneetsa	*Friday*
vtorneek	*Tuesday*	soobota	*Saturday*
sryeda	*Wednesday*	vaskryesyenye	*Sunday*
chyetvyerg	*Thursday*		

To say: *on* Monday/Tuesday/Wednesday... etc. you add 'v' (or 'va' for Tuesday) v panyedyel'neek, va vtorneek, v sryedoo, v chyetvyerg, v pyatneetsoo, v soobotoo, v vaskryesyenye. Some of the endings changed... Spot the differences!

📁 GOOD NEWS GRAMMAR

1 Pronouns – useful!

These are worth learning because you'll need them all the time.

I = ya	*me* = men**ya**	*to/for me* = mnye	*with me* = sa mnoiy
you = vi/vas		*to/for you* = vam	*with you* = s **va**mee
he = on	*him* = yev**o**	*to/for him* = yem**oo**	*with him* = s neem
she = a**na**	*her* = ye**yo**	*to/for her* = yeiy	*with her* = s nyeiy
we = mi	*us* = nas	*to/for us* = nam	*with us* = s **na**mee
they = a**nee**	*them* = eekh	*to for them* = eem	*with them* = s **nee**mee

Learn one row at a time – down or across. Then put each word on a flash card and invest ten minutes a day. By the end of the week you'll know the lot!

2 The future – easy!

If you want to talk about something that is going to happen in the future, you could get away with using the present tense.

Mi **ye**dyem v tsentr.   *We are going to the centre/ We'll go to the centre.*

Sev**o**dnya ya eed**oo** v ryestar**an**.   *Today I am going (will go) to the restaurant.*

But if you want to say: I'll, you'll, or he'll be…, you say: ya b**oo**doo, on b**oo**dyet, vi b**oo**dyete:

Va vt**o**rneek ya b**oo**doo bal'na.   *On Tuesday I will be ill.*

3 I would – would you?

To say **would** in Russian is fairly simple. Let's say: *I would buy…* You'll take the past tense of buy: bought = koop**ee**la – and add the word **bi:**

Ya koop**ee**la bi…   *I would buy…*
A**na** khat**ye**la bi.   *She would like.*
Ba**ree**s skaz**a**l bi…   *Boris would say…*

Easy!

4 Short cut! Leaving out the verb 'to go'

There's another bonus when using n**a**da, m**o**zhna or nyelz**ya**.

When you say that it's necessary, possible or not possible to **go** somewhere you can leave out the *go*: Nam n**a**da v bank. *It's necessary for us (to go) to the bank.* Good shortcut!

4 Being polite

If you ask a question and want to be polite you use the negative.

So, instead of asking: 'Could you help me', you'll say 'You could not help me, (by any chance, could you)?' i.e. Vi nye mozhyete mnye pamoch'?.

Vi nye znayete, gdye nomyer? *You don't know where the number is, (by any chance, do you)?*

5 na, do, po, s, v, za: Lots for the price of a few!

These little words which tell you where things are (also known as prepositions) are most generous: each one has several meanings! Take **na**. It can mean: **on, onto, to, at** and **for**. Here are some others:

do	until, before, as far as	**s**	with, from
po	along, on, according to	**v**	in, into, to, at
za	for, beyond, behind		

Unfortunately, these prepositions do terrible things to the ending of the next word. But don't worry, you'll remember those when you learn your Flash sentences and LEARN BY HEART.

♥ ▭ LEARN BY HEART

This is a telephone call by someone rather self-opinionated… When you have learned it by heart try to act it out in less than a minute.

Vi khateetye eedtee sa mnoiy v ryestaran?

Ya znayu adeen ochyen kharoshiiy ryestaran.
Tam mozhna ochyen vkoosna* yest' ee veeno pryekrasnaye.
Nyet, vi nye khateetye? Pachyemoo nyet? Ya ochyen
eentyeryesnyiy chyelavyek!
Vi menya nye znayete?
No kanyeshna, vi veedeetye** menya po tyelyeveezaroo.
Vi ne mozhyete? Pachyemoo nyet?
Oo vas vazhnaye sveedaniye?
Eta nyevazmozhna!

*vkoosna: *delicious* (the most commonly used word in Russian when praising food)
** veedyet'/veedeetye: *to see/you see*

🔊 📼 SPOT THE KEYS

*This time you are in a department store and ask the sales assistant if the red T-shirt you fancy is also available in a size 40 (*sarakavova razmyera*).*

YOU   Eezveeneetye, pazhalusta, oo vas yest' eta footbolka sarakavova razmyera?

She says 'nyet', then 'meenootachkoo, pazhalusta' and goes into the stockroom. When she comes back, this is what she says:

ANSWER *Nu, oonas takikh* footbolok *kostayotsaochyenmala, oo nas seiychas* tol'ka zhyoltiye sarakavova razmyera. *Noo nasyeshshyoyest* krasniye footbolkee treedtsat' vasmova razmyera. *Ee stil'takoiy,shtoyabiskazala,shto* treedtsat' vasmoiy razmyer vam gadeetsa.

Did you get the keywords? Size 40 was only available in yellow. They have red in 38, which should fit.

💡 SAY IT SIMPLY

When people want to speak Russian but don't dare, it's usually because they are trying to *translate* what they want to say from English into Russian. And when they don't know some of the words, they give up!

With *INSTANT Russian* you work around the words you don't know with the words you do know!

Believe me, with some 400 words you can say anything!

It may not always be very elegant, but you are communicating!

Here are two examples showing you how to say things in a simple way. Words that are not part of the *INSTANT* vocabulary are in **bold**.

You need to **change** your **flight** from Tuesday to Friday.

Mi nye mozhyem **ye**khat' va vtorneek. Mi khateem samalyot v pyatneetsoo.

or

Vtorneek nam nye gadeetsa. Mi khateem **ye**khat' v pyatneetsoo.

Your **watch** is **broken** and you need to have it mended before you leave.

Eezveeneetye, pazhalusta, nada atryemanteeravat' chasi, anee nye rabotayut. Zdyes yest magazeen, gdye mozhna skaryeye atryemanteeravat' eekh?

⬤ ▭▭ LET'S SPEAK RUSSIAN

Here are ten sentences to warm-up, and then onto greater things!

1 Who has said that?
2 I don't know why.
3 You to help? (can I help you?)
4 We have time – on Monday, I believe.
5 I want to drive to Moscow.
6 He would like to know that.
7 Work on Sunday? That's not on!
8 Do you want my number?
9 Chicken for me, please.
10 Yes, of course, I have an appointment for you.

Now pretend you are in Russia with friends who do not speak Russian. They will want you to ask people things in Russian, such as Please ask him...

11 if he knows Edith Palmer.
12 if he is going to the restaurant with us on Tuesday.
13 if she would like meat or fish and fried potato.
14 if they have an appointment today.
15 if they know where the restaurant is.

Now they ask you to tell people things. This time there may be words you don't know, so you have to use your instant words. They say: Please tell her...

16 that the soup is very delicious.
17 that unfortunately the shower is not in working order.
18 that we would like a meal with them.
19 that you are allergic to fish.
20 that Saturday will suit us.

Answers to LET'S SPEAK RUSSIAN

1 Kto skazal eta?
2 Ya ne znayu, pachyemoo.
3 Vam pamoch'?
4 Oo nas vryemya yest' – v panyedyel'neek, kazhyetsa.
5 Ya khachoo yekhat' v Maskvoo.
6 On khatyel bi znat' eta.
7 Rabotat' v vaskryesyenye? Tak nye gadeetsa!
8 Vi khateetye moiy nomyer?
9 Mnye kooreetsoo, pazhalusta.
10 Da, kanyeshna, oo menya sveedaneeye dlya vas.

11 Vi znayete Edeet Palmyer?
12 Vi eedyotye s namee v ryestaran va vtorneek?
13 Vi khateetye myasa eelee riboo s zharyenoiy kartoshkoiy?
14 Oo vas yest' sveedaneeye syevodnya?
15 Vi nye znayete, gdye ryestaran?
16 Soop ochyen vkoosniy.
17 K sazhalyeneeyu doosh nye rabotayet.
18 Mozhna eedtee v ryestaran?
19 On/ana nye yest' riboo.
20 Soobota nam gadeetsa.

☑☒ TEST YOUR PROGRESS

Translate the sentences into Russian.

1 I think the appointment is on Tuesday.

2 Today? No, I am sorry, that is not possible.

3 I must buy many presents.

4 Can('t) you help me, please? I want the number of the doctor.

5 Do(n't) you know where there is a good restaurant?

6 The church is very interesting, it seems.

7 We would like to travel on Monday evening, please.

8 Can I have the menu, please?

9 Excuse me, please, where are the papers?

10 Can one buy fruit here?

11 Do you know his new restaurant?

12 It was wonderful! Thank you very much for the pleasant evening.

13 Why is it necessary for you to see my credit card?

14 It was boring at the theatre on Monday.

15 You see the telephone upstairs by the exit, by the door.

16 We eat chicken or sausage... the fish is too expensive.

17 How does one say in Russian...?

18 Do(n't) you know where here bus? (where there is a bus here?)

19 My husband wants to go to Texas, but I would like to go to New York.

20 He does not know that the new restaurant is behind the church.

How did you go? Another brilliant score on the Progress chart?

5 | WEEK FIVE
DAY-BY-DAY GUIDE

How about 15 minutes on the train, tube or bus, 10 minutes on the way home and 30 minutes before switching on the television...?

Day One
• Read ON THEIR WAY.
• Listen to/Read V POOTEE.
• Listen to/Read the NEW WORDS. Learn 15 or more.

Day Two
• Repeat the dialogue. Learn the harder NEW WORDS.
• Cut out the FLASH WORDS and get stuck in.

Day Three
• Test yourself to perfection on all NEW WORDS.
• Read and learn the GOOD NEWS GRAMMAR (page 48).

Day Four (the tough day)
• Listen to/Read LEARN BY HEART (page 47).
• Cut out and learn the ten FLASH SENTENCES.

Day Five
• Listen to/Read SPOT THE KEYS (page 50).
• Go over LEARN BY HEART.

Day Six
• Listen to/Read LET'S SPEAK RUSSIAN (page 49).
• Translate TEST YOUR PROGRESS.

Day Seven
How is the Progress chart looking? Great? Great!
I bet you don't want a day off... but I insist!

Instant Russian

🔊 ON THEIR WAY

Tom and Kate are travelling across Russia by train, bus and taxi.
They talk to Olga, the ticket clerk, to Jim in the train and to Tatyana
in the bus.

At the station:

Tom   Two tickets to Tver, please.

Olga   There and back?

Tom   There and how (what)? More slowly, please.

Olga   There... and... back.

Tom   To one end (single) only, please. When leaves train and
             from where?

Olga   At 9.45, from fifth platform.

Kate   More quickly (*hurry*), Tom, here are two places, for non-
             smokers. Oh, here is someone here smoking. Excuse me,
             in the train not possible to smoke. These seats are for non-
             smokers. Here to smoke is forbidden.

Jim   Sorry, I don't understand. Ya gavar**yu** only English.

At the bus stop:

Kate   On Sundays few buses. For us it is necessary to wait 20
             minutes. Tom, here are my postcards and letter. Over there
             post box. And I want to take couple of photographs. River
             so beautiful in sun.

Tom   Kate, hurry, are arriving two buses. Both yellow. First
             already full, the other is better.

In the bus:

Tatyana Tickets it is necessary to punch!

Tom   Oh, yes, thank you. To museum it is far?

Tatyana This bus goes not to museum, but to hospital.

In the taxi:

Tom   I very pleased. Taxi not bad and journey not too expensive
             costs.

Kate   To me does not please this car (I don't like), because it old
             and not clean... that's why cheaper. I hope that problems
             will not be.

⋯⟶ Page 46

👁 📼 V POOTEE

Tom and Kate are travelling across Russia by train, bus and taxi.
They talk to Olga, the ticket clerk, to Jim in the train and to Tatyana
in the bus.

Na vakzalye:

Tom	Dva beelyeta v Tvyer, pazhalusta.
Olga	Tooda ee abratna?
Tom	Tooda ee kak? Pamyedlyennyeye, pazhalusta.
Olga	Tooda ... ee... abratna.
Tom	V adeen kanyets tol'ka, pazhalusta. Kakda atkhodeet poyezd ee atkooda?
Olga	V dyevyat sorak pyat, ot pyatoiy platformi.
Kate	Skaryeye, Tom, vot dva myesta, dlya nyekooryashsheekh. Akh, vot kto-ta zdyes kooreet. Eezveeneetye, v poyezdye nyelzya kooreet'. Etee myesta dlya nyekooryashsheekh. Zdyes kooreet' zapryeshayetsa.
Jim	Sorry, I don't understand. Ya gavaryu only English.

Na astanovkye avtoboosa:

Kate	Pa vaskryesyenyam mala avtoboosav. Nam nada zhdat' dvadtsat meenoot. Tom, vot maee atrkitkee ee peesmo. Von tam pachtoviy yashsheek. A ya khachoo snyat' paroo fatagrafeeiy. Ryeka tak kraseeva na solntse.
Tom	Kayeet! Skaryeye, vot dva avtoboosa. Oba zhyoltiye. Pyervyiy oozhye polan, droogoiy loochshye.

V avtoboosye:

Tatyana	Beelyeti nada prakampasteeravat'!
Tom	Akh, da, kanyeshna. Do moozyeya dalyeko?
Tatyana	Etat avtoboos yedyet nye v moozyeiy, a v balneetsoo.

V taksee:

Tom	Ya ochyen davolyen. Taksee nyeplakhoye ee payezdka nye sleeshkam doraga stoeet.
Kate	Mnye ne nraveetsa eta masheena, patamoo shta staraya ee nyecheestaya, vot pachyemoo dyeshyevlye. Ya nadyeyus, shto prablyem nye boodyet.

┈➡ Page 47

Tom There was only this taxi. (Later) Where we? I don't see museum. On left petrol station and station of metro. On right school.

Kate Here is plan of town. To museum, it seems, it is not far... to traffic lights, then right along main street. Why we so slowly travelling? Petrol has finished? Oil has finished? Taxi has broken down? Where my bag? Where mobile 'phone?

Tom Kate, these questions lead me from mind (are driving me crazy). And it is raining. And why police travelling behind us?

abcd... 📼 NEW WORDS

poot/pootee *way, journey*
vakzal *(railway) station*
tooda *to there*
abratna *back/return*
pamyedlyennyeye *a little more slowly*
kanyets *end, direction (one way)*
atkhodeet'/atkhodeet *to leave/it leaves*
poyezd *train*
atkooda *from where*
platforma/platformi *platform*
skaryeye *hurry*
nyekooryashsheekh *non-smokers*
kooreet' *to smoke*
zapryeshayetsa *it is forbidden*
astanovka *bus stop*
pa vaskryesyenyam *on Sundays*
mala *few, little*
zhdat' *to wait*
peesmo *letter*
von tam *over there*
pachtoviy yashsheek *post box*

snyat' *to take (of photographs)*
para/paroo *pair, couple*
fatagrafiya/fatagrafeeiy *photograph/photographs*
ryeka *river*
solntse *sun*
oba *both*
pyervyiy *first*
polan *full*
droogoiy *other, another*
prakampasteeravat' *to punch, clip*
moozyeiy/moozyeya *museum*
(nye)dalyeko *it is (not) far, (not) distant*
etat/ etee *this/these*
balneetsa/balneetsoo *hospital*
nyeplakhoye *not bad*
payezdka *journey*
masheena *car*
patamoo shta *because*
staraya *old*
nyecheestaya *not clean*
nadyeyat'sa/nadyeyus *to hope/ I hope*
taksee *taxi*

Tom   Bila tol'ka eta taksee. *(Pozhye)*. Gdye mi? Ya ne veezhoo
moozyeiy. Nalyeva byenzeenapravachnaya stantseeya ee
stantseeya myetro. Naprava shkola.

Kate   Vot plan gorada. Do moozyeya, kazhetsa, nyedalyeko ... do
svyetafora, patom naprava po glavnaiy ooleetse.
Pachyemoo mi tak myedlyenna yedyem? Byenzeen
koncheelsa? Masla koncheelas? Taksee slomalas? Gdye
maya soomka? Gdye sotaviy tyelyefon?

Tom   Kayeet, etee vaprosee svodyat menya s ooma. Ee eedyot
dozhd. A pachyemoo meeleetseeya yedyet za namee?

eedyot dozhd *it's raining*	byenzeen *petrol*
veedyet'/veezhoo *to see/I see*	koncheelsa/koncheelas *has*
byenzeenapravachnaya	*finished*
stantseeya *petrol station*	masla *oil*
stantseeya myetro *metro station*	slomalas *it has broken down*
shkola *school*	sotaviy tyelyefon *mobile*
plan gorada *plan of the town*	*telephone*
svyetafor/ svyetafora *traffic lights*	svodyat menya s ooma *are*
glavnaiy ooleetse *main street*	*driving me crazy*
myedlyenna *slowly*	meeleetseeya *police*

**TOTAL NEW WORDS: 60
...only 38 words to go!**

 **LEARN BY HEART**

Someone pranged the car and someone else is getting suspicious!

Masheena tol'ka nyemnozhka slamalas...
Zavtra nam mozhna smatryet' tyennees?
Oo myenya dva beelyeta na match.
Ya khachoo veedyet' novykh amyereekanskeekh tyenneeseestav.*
Mozhna yekhat' tooda na myetro?
Eelee loochshye na avtoboosye, patamoo shta on yedyet pryama
na stadeeon.
Avtoboos? Myetro? Pachyemoo? Mnye ne nraveetsa garadskoiy
transport.
Oo nas kraseevaya masheena.
Da, no... vchyera, kagda ya yekhal v gorad, ya nye veedyel svyetafor...
no masheena tol'ka nyemnozhka slamalas...

---

tyenneeseestav*: *tennis players*

⊙⌨ GOOD NEWS GRAMMAR

1 nraveetsa – to like – or not like

Think how often you use this in English: I like this – you don't like that – do you like…?

In Russian you use nraveetsa, but it is a bit of a strange construction. Think of it as *something that is pleasing to you*:

I like the car –
  To me is pleasing the car.   Mnye nraveetsa masheena.
We don't like the car –
  To us is not pleasing the car.   Nam ne nraveetsa masheena.
Do you like to work? –
  To you is pleasing to work?   Vam nraveetsa rabotat'?

Once you get used to *is pleasing* it's quite simple really. Just remember nraveetsa.

2 Saying the opposite – just add nye

This an easy way to double your vocabulary! As opposed to learning two words just use one and add nye:

Tooalyeti cheestiye.   *The toilets are clean.*
Tooalyetee nyecheestiye.   *The toilets are dirty.*
Eta nyekraseeviy gorad.   *It is an ugly (not beautiful) town.*

3 Another short cut – Can and can't

In such common phrases as 'Can you hear…?' or 'Can't you see…?' the Russians will leave out the *can* or *can't* altogether:

Ya ne slishoo yevo.   *I can't hear him.*
Vi veedeetye tyelyeveezar?   *Can you see the television?*

Makes it easier, doesn't it?

4 No more new grammar!

After this week there's no more new grammar. After all, you decided on *INSTANT* **Russian** because you wanted a starter kit – not a complicated textbook.

If you remember all the grammar notes, words and phrases in the book you'll have done very well indeed.

◯ 📼 LET'S SPEAK RUSSIAN

A ten-point warm-up: I give you an answer and you ask me a question as if you did not hear the words in CAPITAL LETTERS very well.

Example Veektar ZDYES.   *Question* Gdye Veektar?

1 Sotaviy tyelyefon OO MENYA V SOOMKYE.
2 SHKOLA von tam.
3 Poyezd atkhodeet V TREE CHASA.
4 TOM khochyet gavareet' s Bareesam Eevanaveechyem.
5 Beelyet tooda ee abratna stoeet 80 ROOBLYEIY.
6 Mnye ne nraveetsa masheena, PATAMOO SHTA ona ochyen staraya.
7 Vi yedyetye v Angleeyu NA SAMALYOTYE.
8 Ya ooveedyel(a) SVYETAFOR.
9 DA, mnye nraveetsa gasteeneetsa.
10 Mnye nraveetsa MOOZYEIY.

Now answer starting with '**da**':

11 Vi znayete novyiy magazeen?
12 Vi yedyetye syeiychas v balneetso?
13 Vam nraveetsa ryeka?
14 Vi veedeetye astanovkoo avtoboosa?

Here are three things that you want to refer to. But you don't know what they are called in Russian. Explain them using the words you know:

15 a refrigerator
16 a holiday
17 a kennel

Answers to LET'S SPEAK RUSSIAN

1 Gdye sotavyiy tyelyefon?
2 Shto eta von tam?
3 Kakda atkhodeet poyezd?
4 Kto khochyet gavereet' s Bareesam Eevanaveechyem?
5 Skol'ka stoeet beelyet tooda ee abratna?
6 Pachyemoo vam ne nraveetsa masheena?
7 Kak vi yedyete v Angleeyu?
8 Shto vi ooveedyelee?
9 Vam nraveetsa gasteeneetsa?
10 Shto vam nraveetsa?
11 Da, ya znayu noviy magazeen.
12 Da, ya yedoo syeiychas v balneetsoo.
13 Da, mnye nraveetsa ryeka.
14 Da, ya veezhoo astanovkoo avtoboosa.
15 Myesta, gdye kholadna, dlya malaka, myasa, sira
16 Vryemya, kagda vi nye rabotayetye.
17 Dom dlya sabakee, kagda mi v otpooskye.

⚙ ▭ SPOT THE KEYS

This time you are planning a trip in the country and want to have some idea what the weather will be like. This is what you could ask:

You   Eezveeneetye, pazhalusta, vi nye mozhyetye mnye skazat', kakaya zavtra boodyet pagoda?

Answer   *Eezveeneetye, ya nye znayu, no kagdayasmatryel* pragnoz pagodi po tyelyeveezaroo, *skazalee, shto pagoda* myedlyenna *myenyayetsa.* Zavtra *boodyet* kholadna – *vosem gradoosav, s nebolsheemvyetram ee* dozhd boodyet k vyechyeroo.

He doesn't know, but according to the TV something slow is happening and it will be cold tomorrow, 8 degrees, with rain in the evening.

✔✗ TEST YOUR PROGRESS

1 I don't like this bag. The other bag was better.
2 How much does (the) ticket cost – return?
3 What did you say? Slowly, please.
4 I know that in America petrol is cheaper.
5 In (the) underground it is forbidden to smoke.
6 I cannot wait, I have (an) appointment at 11 o'clock.
7 Is this (the) letter box? (A) yellow letterbox?
8 Hello, we are 30km from Novgorod. Is that (the) petrol station?
9 Which is cheaper? (The) bus or (the) metro?
10 Today it is very cold. I hope that it will rain.
11   The traffic light was red, not green. That's why they're both in hospital.
12 She was at (the) petrol station today on Monday and Tuesday. The car drinks petrol!
13 Where here dry cleaner? By me oil on T-shirt 'Armani'.
14 Our flat (is) behind (the) main street, by (the) bus stop.
15 We are by police (at the police station), because we do not know where our mobile phone (is).
16 It is necessary to buy (the) tickets now, because they cheaper.
17 I like your car. Was it very expensive?
18 Can you help us, please? Can one eat here by river?

If you know all your words you should score over 90%!

6 WEEK SIX
DAY-BY-DAY GUIDE

This is your last week! Need I say more?

Day One
- Read IN THE AIRPORT.
- Listen to/Read V AERAPARTOO.
- Listen to/Read NEW WORDS. There are only a handful!

Day Two
- Repeat V AERAPARTOO. Learn all NEW WORDS.
- Work with the FLASH WORDS and FLASH SENTENCES.

Day Three
- Test yourself on the FLASH SENTENCES.
- No more GOOD NEWS GRAMMAR! Try this quiz instead (page 56).

Day Four
- Listen to/Read and learn DASVEEDANIYA (page 55)!
- Listen to/Read SPOT THE KEYS (page 57).

Day Five
- Listen to/Read LET'S SPEAK RUSSIAN (page 58).
- Read SAY IT SIMPLY (page 57).

Day Six
- Your last TEST YOUR PROGRESS! Go for it!

Day Seven

Congratulations!

**You have successfully completed the course
and can now speak**

INSTANT Russian!

IN THE AIRPORT

Tom and Kate are on their way back to Birmingham. They are in the departure lounge of Moscow airport.

Tom On Monday for us it is necessary will be to work. Terrible! I want (to go) to Italy or to Hawaii! No one in my firm knows where I (am).

Kate And in *my* firm? They know (the) number of telephone of my mother, and she knows the number of our mobile telephone...

Tom Yes, yes, I know. Well, perhaps at Christmas, (a) week in the snow or let's go on (a) ship to Madeira. But I want to buy (a) newspaper downstairs... Kate! There is Yuriy Zhivago!

Yuriy Hello! How are things? What you here are doing? This is my wife, Nancy. Already (the) end of your holiday? Well, how all went? (How did it go?)

Kate Splendidly! (wonderful). We much saw and too much ate. Now we well know Moscow, and Yalta, and Saint Petersburg...

Yuriy Next year for you it is necessary to (go to) Novgorod! Mrs Walker, my wife wants to buy a book for our computer. You [not] can help her (Could you help her at all?) Mr Walker, you have a newspaper. Give, please, (the) sport. Then I invite you to (the) bar.

At the airport kiosk:

Kate Here nothing suitable there is [not]. You also going to England?

Nancy No, we are going to Saint Petersburg. Mother of Yuriy lives there. Our children were by her for two weeks. By us (we have) boy and three girls. Tomorrow we are going to Novgorod on the train. It is cheaper.

Kate Your husband works in (a) bank?

Nancy Yes, his work (is) interesting, but money not big. To our Lada already nine years (our Lada is already nine years old) and by us (we have) old, small flat. [In] this year much (we) have repaired. My parents and my girlfriend (are) in

⋯⟶ Page 54

🎵 📼 V AERAPARTOO

Tom and Kate are on their way back to Birmingham. They are in the departure lounge of Moscow airport.

Tom   V panyedyelneek nam nada boodyet rabotat'. **Oo**zhas! Ya khach**oo** v Eetaleeyu **ee**lee na Gav**ai**yee! Neekt**o** v ma**yeiy** feermye nye znayet, gdye ya.

Kate   A v ma**yeiy** feerm**ye**? An**ee** znayut n**o**myer tyelef**o**na ma**yeiy** mami, a ana znayet n**o**myer nashyeva s**o**tavava tyelyef**o**na.

Tom   Da, da, znayu. Noo, m**o**zhyet bit' na Razhdyestv**o**, nyed**ye**lyu v snyeg**oo ee**lee pa**ye**dyem na tyeplakh**o**dye na Mad**ye**iyr**oo**. A ya khach**oo** koop**ee**t' gaz**ye**too vneez**oo**... Kate! Vot **Yu**riy Zhivago!

Yuriy   Zdravstv**oo**eetye! Kak dyel**a**? Shto vi zdyes d**ye**layetye? Eta ma**ya** zhyen**a**, Nancy. **Oo**zhye kan**ye**ts v**a**shyeva **o**tp**oo**ska? Noo, kak vsyo prashl**o**?

Kate   Vyeleekal**ye**pna! Mi mn**o**ga v**ee**dyelee ee sl**ee**shkam mn**o**ga **ye**lee.   Syeiychas mi kharash**o** znayem ee Maskv**oo ee Ya**ltoo ee Sankt-Pyetyerb**oo**rg...

Yuriy   V sl**ye**dooyushshyem gad**oo** vam n**a**da v N**o**vgarad! Gaspazh**a** Walker, ma**ya** zhyen**a** kh**o**chyet koop**ee**t' kn**ee**goo dlya nashyeva kamp**yu**tyera. Vi nye m**o**zhyetye yeiy pam**o**ch'? Gaspad**ee**n Walker, oo vas gaz**ye**ta. D**a**eeytye, pazh**a**lusta, sport. Pat**o**m preeglash**a**yu vas v bar.

*V aerapart**oo**, oo ke**eo**ska:*

Kate   Zdyes neechyev**o** padkhad**ya**shshyeva nyet. Vi t**o**zhye **ye**dyetye v Angl**ee**yu?

Nancy   Nyet, mi **ye**dyem v Sankt-Pyetyerb**oo**rg. M**a**ma **Yu**ri zheev**yo**t tam. N**a**shee d**ye**tee b**i**lee oo nye**yo** dve n**ye**dyelee. Oo nas m**a**lcheek ee tree d**ye**vachkee. Z**a**vtra mi **ye**dyem v N**o**vgarad na p**o**yezdye. **E**ta dyeshy**e**vlye.

Kate   Vash m**oo**zh rab**o**tayet v b**a**nkye?

Nancy   Da, yev**o** rab**o**ta eent**ye**ry**e**snaya, no d**ye**ng**ee** nyeb**a**lsh**ee**ye N**a**shy**ei**y L**a**dye o**o**zh**ye** d**ye**vyat lyet ee oo nas st**a**raya, m**a**lyenkaya kvart**ee**ra. V etam gad**oo** mn**o**ga atry**e**mant**ee**raval**ee**.   M**a**ee rad**ee**tyelee ee padr**oo**ga v

┅┅➡ Page 55

(the) USA and we often write letters. I would like (to go) to America, but too expensive costs.

Kate   But by you (you have) (a) beautiful house in Greece.

Nancy   (A) house in Greece? I never [not] was in Greece (I have never been to Greece). When by us (we have) (a) holiday, we go to friend('s), at Chyelyabeensk.

Tom   Kate, hurry, for us it is time (to go). What said Mrs Zhivago?

Kate   Wait, Tom, wait!

abcd... 🔊 NEW WORDS

Eetaleeya/Eetaleeyu   *Italy*
Gavaiyee   *Hawaii*
mami/mama   *mother*
Razhdyestvo   *Christmas*
snyeg/snyegoo   *snow*
payedyem   *let's go*
tyeplakhod/tyeplakhodye   *ship*
Madyeiyra/Madyeiyroo   *Madeira*
vneezoo   *downstairs*
kak dyela?   *how are things?*
prashlo   *it went by, passed*
vyeleekalyepna   *splendid(ly), great, wonderful(ly)*
yelee   *we/they ate*
v slyedooyushshyem [etam] gadoo   *next [this] year*
kneego   *book*
daeeytye   *give!*
preeglashat'/preeglashayu   *to invite/I invite*
bar   *bar*
neechyevo   *nothing*

padkhadyashshiiy/ padkhadyashshyeva   *suitable*
zheevyot   *lives*
dyetee   *children*
dvye (f)   *two*
malcheek   *boy*
dyevachka/dyevachkee   *(little) girl/girls*
dyeshyevlye   *cheaper*
moozh   *husband*
Lada/Ladoo   *Lada*
lyet   *of years*
malyenkiiy/malyenkaya   *small*
S-SHA   *USA*
peeshyem   *we write*
chasta   *often*
peesma   *letters*
neekakda nye   *never*
droog/droogoo   *friend*
para   *it is time (to go)*
padazhdee!   *wait!*

TOTAL NEW WORDS: 38
TOTAL RUSSIAN WORDS LEARNED: 379
EXTRA WORDS: 76

GRAND TOTAL: 455

S-SHA ee mi chasta peeshyem peesma. Ya ochyen khatyela bi v Amyereekoo, no sleeshkam doraga stoeet.

Kate No oo vas kraseevyiy dom v Gryetsee-ee.

Nancy Dom v Gryetsee-ee? Ya neekakda nye bila v Gryetsee-ee. Kakda oo nas otpoosk, mi yedyem k droogoo v Chyelyabeensk.

Tom Kate! Skaryeye, nam para! Shto skazala gaspazha Zhivago?

Kate Padazhdee, Tom, padazhdee!

💙 📼 LEARN BY HEART

This is your last dialogue to LEARN BY HEART. Give it your best! You now have six prize-winning party pieces, and a large store of everyday sayings which will be very useful.

Dasveedaneeya!

Kate Barees Vadeemaveech, gavareet Kate Walker, ya v aeraportoo v Maskvye.
Da, oozhye kanyets nashyeva otpooska ee nasheekh dyenyeg tozhye!
Spaseeba balshoye za ochyen preeyatniiy vyechyer!
Tom khochyet gavareet' s vamee.

Tom Zdravstvooeetye, Barees Vadeemaveech... Kak? Vi khateetye koopeet' oba?
Oo meoyeiy feermi yest' vash e-mail? Vyeleekalyepna. Spaseeba balshoye!
V slyedooyushshyem gadoo?... Kate khochyet v Eetaleeyu, no myne nraveetsa Rasseeya.*
S Edith Palmyer? Akh, Bozhye moiy, nyet, nyet! Nash samalyot zhdyot... Noo... Dasveedaneeya!

*Rasseeya: *Russia*

 GOOD NEWS GRAMMAR

There's no more grammar this week just a couple of interesting points.

1 Double negative

The Russians love to say **ny**et so they sometimes say it twice!:

> Neek**to** nye zn**a**yet, gdye ya.   *No one not knows where I am.*
> Ya neek**a**gda nye bil**a**   *I never not was in Greece.*
> v Gry**e**tsee-ee.

2 Surnames

Yuriy Baran**a**v… and his wife, Mrs Baran**a**va. In Russian, a man's surname usually ends in a consonant and a woman's in the letter 'a' (thus **A**nna Kar**y**en**ee**na's husband's surname was Kar**y**en**ee**n).

3 Quiz

And now for some light relief: the end of course quiz!

No marks for this one – just a pat on the back!

1 In which city would you find the Kry**e**ml'?
   a Sankt-Pyetyerb**oo**rg   c **Y**alta
   b Maskv**a**   d Vladeevast**o**k

2 How would you say 12 o'clock in Russian?
   a dva chas**a**   c dven**a**dtsat chas**o**v
   b dv**a**dtsat chas**o**v

3 How would you greet someone if you met them in the evening?
   a d**o**braye **oo**tra   c dasveed**a**neeya
   b d**o**briiy dyen   d d**o**briiy v**ye**chyer

4 If you were a vegetarian, which of these would you not eat?
   a m**ya**sa   c tort
   b fr**oo**kti   d kart**o**shka

5 When do you celebrate Christmas in Russia?
   a 24 dyekabr**ya**   c 31 dyekabr**ya**
   b 25 dyekabr**ya**   d 6 yanvar**ya**

6 If you wanted to apologise, what would you say?
   a kharahsh**o**   c oozh**a**sna
   b eezveen**ee**tye   d kan**ye**shna

7 When does *Dyed maroz* (the Russian version of Father Christmas) bring presents?
   a 24 dyekabr**ya**   c 31 dyekabr**ya**
   b 25 dyekabr**ya**   d 6 yanvar**ya**

8 What does 'shto vam' mean?
- a Where are you?
- b What would you like?
- c Where do you work?

9 How do you say in Russian 'I understand'?
- a ya paneem**a**yu
- b ya zn**a**yu
- c ya khach**oo**
- d ya mag**oo**

10 What do Russians say when they really don't approve of what you want to do?
- a tak m**o**zhna
- b tak nyel'z**ya**
- c tak n**a**da
- d tak ne gad**ee**tsa

You'll find the answers on page 63.

SPOT THE KEYS

Here are two final practice rounds. If you have the cassette, close the book NOW. Find the key words and try to get the gist of it. Then check on page 63.

This is what you might ask a taxi driver:

YOU Skol'ka meen**oot** do aerapart**oo** ee sk**o**lka st**o**eet?

ANSWER *Eta zaveeseet ot tavo, kakda vi yedyetye. Abichna payezdka dleetsa dvadtsat meenoot, no yeslee vi khateetye yekhat' v chasee-peek ee probkee vyezdye, payezdka mozhyet dleetsa sorak pyat meenoot... asobyenna po pyatneetsam, kagda khoozhye vsyevo. Skol'ka stoeet? Abichna ot treedtsatee do pyateedyesyatee rooblyeiy.*

SAY IT SIMPLY

1 You are staying in a hotel in Russia. The television and the shower are both broken. Report it – you want to use both!

2 You are at the airport, about to catch your flight home when you realise that you have left a bag behind in the room of your hotel. You phone the hotel reception and ask for it to be sent on to you.

What would you say in these two cases? Say it then write it down. Then see the two examples on page 63. Yours can be different and even simpler, based solely on your *INSTANT* vocabulary. Give it a go!

● ▭ LET'S SPEAK RUSSIAN

Here's a quick warm-up. Answer the questions using the words in brackets.

1 On koopeel dom v Marbella? (da, panyedyelneek)
2 Skolka lyet vi rabotalee v bankye? (pyat)
3 Kakda vi gavareelee s vashyeiy feermaiy? (vchyera)
4 Pachyemoo vam nada atryemanteeravat' vashoo masheenoo? (patamoo shta, staraya)
5 On bil snachala v gasteeneetsye? (nyet, v kvarteerye)

Now practise your verbs with 'nada', 'nyelzya' and 'para':

6 Oozhas! Kvarteera ochyen staraya... (You mustn't buy it).
7 Skaryeye! Oozhye dyevyat chasov... (It's time for us to go).
8 ... (You must mend the television), yeslee on nye rabotayet.

Finish off the sentences, using phrases which start with 'shto' and 'patamoo shta':

9 Maya padrooga skazala... (that already end of holiday).
10 Ana tozhye skazala... (that she really likes Moscow).
11 Maya zhyena khochyet skazat'... (that she has (a) cold).
12 Moiy moozh gavareet, shto on nye mozhyet v tyeatr... (because he is working).
13 Olga tozhye ne mozhyet v tyeatr... (because she is on holiday).
14 Moiy droog gavareet... (that she is very beautiful).
15 On gavareet tozhye... (that he wants her telephone number).

Answers to LET'S SPEAK RUSSIAN

1 Da, on koopeel dom v Marbella v panyedyelneek.
2 Ya rabotal/rabotala v bankye pyat lyet.
3 Ya gavareel/gavareela s mayeiy feermaiy vchyera.
4 Nam nada atryemanteeravat' nashoo masheenoo, patamoo shta ana staraya.
5 Nyet, snachala on bil v kvarteerye.
6 Oozhas! Kvarteera ochyen staraya. Vam nyelzya koopeet' yeyo.
7 Skaryeye! Oozhye dyevyat chasov. Nam para eedtee.
8 Vam nada atryemanteeravat' tyelyeveezar, yeslee on nye rabotayet.
9 Maya padrooga skazala, shto oozhye kanyets otpooska.
10 Ana tozhye skazala, shto yeiy ochyen nraveetsa Maskva.
11 Maya zhyena khochyet skazat', shto oo nyeyo prastooda.
12 Moiy moozh gavareet, shto on nye mozhyet v tyeatr, patamoo shta on rabotayet.
13 Olga tozhye ne mozhyet v tyeatr, patamoo shta ana v otpooskye.
14 Moiy droog gavareet, shto ana ochyen kraseevaya.
15 On gavareet tozhye, shto on khochyet yeyo nomyer tyelyefona.

✔✘ TEST YOUR PROGRESS

A lot of INSTANT verbs have been crammed into this. But don't panic – it looks worse than it is. Go for it – you'll do brilliantly!

1 I like writing letters because I have (a) new computer.
2 How are you? You have (a) problem? To help you? Can I help you?
3 Excuse me, do you have the number of (her) mobile?
4 I like (the) Crimea (Krim). It is never cold there.
5 The other case is in (the) bus. Have you got (the) brown bag?
6 Where will you be at Christmas?
7 Who wants fish and who wants meat?
8 He has my telephone number. He often rings me.
9 Quickly! Where is (the) ticket? The train is coming!
10 Don't you know that (the) airport is always open?
11 My holiday is very important. I want (to go) to Italy.
12 Have you seen Olga in the newspaper? Without (her) husband?
13 Your mother is very pleasant. Her walnut cake is delicious!
14 We must work. We have three boys and two girls. Very expensive costs!
15 Excuse me, where is it possible to repair (the) car?
16 I know him. He always goes shopping with (his) dog.
17 Who said it is impossible (one cannot) here to smoke?
18 We are travelling to (the) airport by taxi, then to Dallas by 'plane.
19 I would like to speak to (the) waiter. Where is (the) bill?
20 I am sorry, but this is the end of *INSTANT* **Russian**.

Check your answers on page 63. Then enter your final excellent score on the Progress chart and write out your certificate!

🔑 ANSWERS

How to score

From a total of 100%:

- Subtract 1% for each wrong or missing word.
- Subtract 1% for the wrong form of the verb, like **yed**yem when it should be **yed**oo.
- Subtract 1% for mixing up the pronouns such as vi, vam, **v**amee.

There are no penalties for:

- Wrong or different ending of the word, e.g. kamp**yu**tyer – kamp**yu**tyera.
- Picking the wrong 'version' of the word, e.g. noviy – novim.
- Picking the wrong word where there are two of similar meaning, e.g. **no** and **a**.
- Wrong spelling, as long as you can say the word! e.g. ee**yu**n – iy**oo**n.
- Different word order.

100% LESS YOUR PENALTIES WILL GIVE YOUR WEEKLY SCORE

For each test, correct your mistakes. Then read the corrected answers aloud twice.

WEEK 1 – TEST YOUR PROGRESS

1 Men**ya** zavo**ot** Frank Lukas.
2 Zdr**a**vstvooeetye, mi – V**ee**ktar ee **O**lga.
3 Ya t**o**zhe eez **O**mska.
4 V aktyabr**ye** ya bil/bil**a** v Maskv**ye**.
5 Mi bil**ee** tree g**o**da v Am**ye**reekye.
6 L**o**ndan st**o**eet dor**a**ga.
7 Eezveen**ee**tye, paz**ha**lusta, gdye vi rab**o**tayetye?
8 Vi rab**o**tayete v Manch**ye**styerye?
9 Vi V**ee**ktar Eezm**ai**ylav eez T**o**mska?
10 Kvart**ee**ra v N**o**vgaradye **o**chyen b**a**lshaya.
11 Meen**oo**tachkoo, paz**ha**lusta, oo men**ya** b**o**lshye d**e**neg.
12 Tam yest tyelyef**o**n? Nyet, k sazhal**ye**niyu.
13 Ya v **Ya**ltye byez s**i**na.
14 F**ee**rma b**a**lshaya?
15 Myersyed**ye**s dor**a**ga st**o**eet?
16 V apr**ye**lye L**o**ndan **o**chyen kras**ee**viiy.
17 Oo ny**e**vo v toorag**ye**ntstvye padr**o**oga.
18 K sazhal**ye**niyu rab**o**ta **o**chyen sk**oo**chnaya.
19 Rab**o**ta **o**chyen khar**o**shaya, no otp**oo**sk l**oo**chshye.
20 M**a**ya doch vsegd**a** zvan**ee**t.

YOUR SCORE: _____ %

WEEK 2 – TEST YOUR PROGRESS

1 Ya pyu mnoga shampanskava.
2 Skol'ka stoeet zavtrak, pazhalusta.
3 Zdyes yest' tooragyenstva?
4 Oo vas yest' stol? V syem pyatnadtsat?
5 Ya khachoo peet' kofye.
6 Moiy otpoosk v Floreedye bil loochshye.
7 Gdye kharoshaya gasteeneetsa?
8 Telefonniy shyot, pazhalusta.
9 Mi bilee v Sankt-Pyetyerboorgye v maye.
10 Moiy dom sleeshkam balshoiy.
11 V katoram chasoo vi v Maskvoo zavtra?
12 Ya tam s vosmee do pyatee.
13 Eezveeneetye, pazhalusta. Gdye tooalyety, pryama?
14 Mi khateem yekhat' v Osla v yanvarye, no sleeshkam kholadna.
15 Eta stoeet bolshye dyenyeg?
16 Zavtra, gdye vi v dyesyat treedtsat?
17 Oozhasna. Nomyer ochyen doraga stoeet.
18 Zdyes mozhna peet' kofye syeiychas? Oo vas yest' myesta?
19 Oo nas malyenkiiy dom v Amyereekye, no on ochyen doraga stoeet.
20 Dasveedaniya, mi yedyem v Yaltoo.

YOUR SCORE: _____ %

WEEK 3 – TEST YOUR PROGRESS

1 Gdye pradavyets?
2 Gdye mozhna koopeet' bootyerbrodi?
3 Kakda vam nada v Angleeyu syevodnya? V syem chasov?
4 Mi ooveedyelee eta vchyera po tyelyeveezaroo.
5 Seiychas magazeeni atkriti, kazhetsa.
6 Zdyes yest ooneevyermag eelee soopyermarkyet.
7 Eezveeneetye, vi tozhye eedyotye na pochtoo?
8 Gdye vi koopeelee angleeskooyu gazyetoo?
9 Vi khateetye kofye eelee chaiy?
10 Syevodnya pagoda plakhaya. Nyelzya v Novgarad.
11 Eta vsyo? Eta bila nyedoraga.
12 Markee stoeelee pyatnadtsat roobleiy.
13 Mi preeneemayem kryedeetniye kartochkee.
14 Treesta gram sira sleeshkam mnoga? Nyet, nyet prablyem.
15 Yest' novaya kheemcheestka bleezka atsyuda.
16 Oo vas yest' pakyeteek dlya moeiy footbolkee, pazhalusta?
17 Ya zdyes ooveedyela aptyekoo, kazhetsa.
18 Bozhye moiy! Avtoboos nye rabotayet ee Myersyedyes tozhye nye rabotayet!
19 Vi ooveedyelee footbolkoo? Gdye vi koopeelee yeyo?
20 Pyatsot rooblyeiy, no oo myenya tolka dollari.

YOUR SCORE: _____ %

WEEK 4 – TEST YOUR PROGRESS

1 Ya doomayu, shto sveedaneeiye va vtorneek.
2 Sevodnya? Nyet, eezveeneetye, eta nyevazmozhna.
3 Mnye nada koopeet' mnoga padarkav.
4 Vi nye mozhyete mnye pamoch', pazhalusta? Ya khachoo nomyer vracha.
5 Vi nye znayete, gdye yest' kharoshiy ryestaran.
6 Tserkav ochyen eentyeryesnaya, kazhetsa.
7 Mi khatyelee bi yekhat' v panyedyelneek vyechyeram.
8 Mozhna menyu, pazhalusta?
9 Eezveeneetye, pazhalusta, gdye boomagee?
10 Zdyes mozhna koopeet' frookti?
11 Vi znayete yevo noviy ryestaran?
12 Eta bila prekrasna. Spaseeba balshoye za ochyen preeyatniy vyechyer.
13 Pachyemoo vam nada veedyet' mayu kryedeetnooyu kartachkoo?
14 Bila skoochna v tyeatrye v panyedyelneek.
15 Vi veedeetye tyelyefon navyerkhoo, okala vikhada, okala dvyeree.
16 Mi yedeem kooreetsoo eelee kalbasoo... riba sleeshkam doraga stoeet.
17 Kak pa-roosskee...?
18 Vi nye znayete, gdye zdyes avtoboos?
19 Moiy moozh khochyet yekhat' v Tyekhas, a ya khatyela bi yekhat' v Nyu Eeyork.
20 On nye znayet, shto novyi ryestaran za tserkvyu.

> YOUR SCORE: _____ %

WEEK 5 – TEST YOUR PROGRESS

1 Mnye nye nraveetsa eta soomka. Drugaya soomka bila loochshye.
2 Skolka stoeet beelyet – tooda ee abratna?
3 Shto vi skazalee? Pamyedlyennyeye, pazhalusta.
4 Ya znayu, shto v Amyereekye byenzeen dyeshyevlye.
5 V myetro kooreet' zapryeshshayetsa.
6 Ya ne magoo zhdat'. Oo myenya sveedaneeye v adeenadtsat' chasov.
7 Eta pachtoviy yashsheek? Zhyoltiy yashsheek?
8 Allo, mi v treedtsatee keelamyetrakh ot Novgarada. Eta byenzeenapravachnaya stantseeya?
9 Shto dyeshyevlye? Avtoboos eelee myetro?
10 Syevodnya ochyen kholadna. Nadyeyus, dozhd boodyet.
11 Svyetafor bil krasnyiy, nye zyelyonyiy. Vot pachyemoo anee oba v balneetsye.
12 Ana bila na byenzeenapravachnoy stantsee-ee v panyedyelneek ee va vtorneek. Masheena pyot byenzeen!
13 Gdye zdes kheemcheestka? Oo myenya masla na footbolkye 'Armanee'.
14 Nasha kvarteera za glavnaiy ooleetseiy, oo (or okala) astanovkee avtoboosa.
15 Mi oo meeleetsee-ee, patamoo shta mi nye znayem, gdye nash sotaviy tyelyefon.
16 Nada koopeet' beelyetee syeiychas, patamoo shta anee dyeshyevlye.
17 Mnye nraveetsa vasha masheena. Ana ochyen doraga stoeela?
18 Vi nye mozhyetye nam pamoch'? Mozhna zdyes yest' okala ryekee?

> YOUR SCORE: _____ %

WEEK 6 – TEST YOUR PROGRESS

1 Mnye nraveetsa peesat' pees'ma, patamoo shta oo myenya noviiy kampyutyer.
2 Kak dyela? Oo vas prablyema? Vam pamoch'?
3 Eezveeneetye, oo vas yest' nomyer yeyo satavova tyelyefona?
4 Mnye nraveetsa Krim. Tam neekagda nye kholadna.
5 Droogoiy chyemadan v avtoboosye. Oo vas kareechnyevaya soomka?
6 Gdye vi boodyete na Razhdyestvo?
7 Kto khochyet riboo ee kto khochyet myasa?
8 Oo nyevo moiy nomyer tyelyefona. On chasta zvaneet mnye.
9 Skaryeye! Gdye beelyet? Poyezd eedyot!
10 Vi ne znayete, shto aeraport vsyegda atkrit?
11 Moiy otpoosk ochyen vazhniy. Ya khachoo v Eetaleeyu.
12 Vi veedyelee Olgoo v gazyetye? Byez moozha?
13 Vasha mama ochyen preeyatnaya. Yeyo aryekhaviy tort ochyen vkoosniy!
14 Nam nada rabotat'. Oo nas tree malcheeka ee adna dyevachka. Ochyen doraga stoeet!
15 Eezveeneetye, gdye mozhna atryemanteeravat' masheenoo?
16 Mi yevo znayem. On vsyegda dyelayet pakoopkee s sabakaiy.
17 Kto skazal, shto zdyes nyelzya kooreet'?
18 Mi yedyem v aeroport na taksee, patom v Dallas na samalyotye.
19 Ya khachoo gavareet' s afeetseeantam. Gdye shyot?
20 Eezveeneetye, no eta kanyets *INSTANT Russian.*

YOUR SCORE: _____ %

SPOT THE KEYS

Depends when you travel. Usually 20 minutes, but at rush hour when traffic jams everywhere journey might last 45 minutes. Cost usually between 30 and 50 roubles.

SAY IT SIMPLY

1 Eezveeneetye, pazhalusta, ya v nomyere 222. Tam tyelyeveezar nye rabotayet ee doosh nye rabotayet. Pazhalusta, eekh nada atryemanteeravat'. Ya nadyeyus, shto vi mozhyetye mnye pamoch'!
2 Zdravstvooeetye. Gavareet Kayeet Green. Ya bila v vashyeiy gasteeneetse, v nomyere... K sazhalyeneeyu ya oozhye v aerapartoo, a maya soomka v nomyere. Pazhalusta, mayu soomkoo nada v Angleeyu. Gasteeneetsa znayet, gdye ya zheevoo. Spaseeba balshoye.

QUIZ

1b 2c 3d 4a 5d 6b 7c 8b 9a 10b/d

⚡HOW TO USE THE FLASHCARDS

The FLASHCARDS have been voted the best part of this course! Learning words and sentences can be tedious, but with flashcards it's quick and good fun.

This is what you do:

When the Day-by-day guide tells you to use the cards, cut them out. There are 18 FLASH WORDS and 10 FLASH SENTENCES for each week. Each card has a little number on it telling you to which week it belongs, so you won't cut out too many cards at a time or muddle them up later on.

First, try to learn the words and sentences by looking at both sides of the cards. Then, when you have a rough idea, start testing yourself. That's the fun bit. Look at the English, say the Russian, and then check. Make a pile for 'correct' and one for 'wrong' and 'don't know'. When all the cards are used up, start again with the 'wrong' pile and try to whittle it down until you get all of them right.

You can also play it 'backwards' by starting with the Russian face-up.

Keep the cards in a little box or put an elastic band around them. Take them with you on the bus, the train, to the hairdresser or the dentist.

If you find the paper too flimsy, photocopy the words and sentences onto card before cutting them up. You could also buy some plain card and stick them on or simply copy them out.

The 18 FLASH WORDS for each week are there to start you off. Convert the rest of the NEW WORDS to FLASH WORDS, too. It's well worth it!

> **FLASHCARDS for INSTANT LEARNING:**
> **DON'T LOSE THEM – USE THEM!**

1	1
eezvee**nee**tye	pazh**a**lusta
1	1
oo nas	da
1	1
mi	nyet
1	1
ya	**ye**doo
1	1
vi	rab**o**tayu
1	1
gdye	rab**o**ta

please **1**	excuse me **1**
yes **1**	by us (we have) **1**
no **1**	we **1**
I go (travel) **1**	I **1**
I work **1**	you **1**
work, job **1**	where **1**

kharoshaya [1]	dyeneg [1]
oo myenya [1]	eta [1]
bank [1] банк	v otpooskye [1]
nada [2]	skol'ka [2]
rooblyeiy [2]	na chyelovyeka [2]
kryedeetniye [2] kartachkee	zavtrak [2]

money [1]	good [1]
it is [1]	I have [1]
on holiday [1]	bank [1]
how much/ how many [2]	it is necessary [2]
per person [2]	roubles [2]
breakfast [2]	credit cards [2]

mi khat**ee**m ^{2}	m**o**zhna ^{2}
chaiy ^{2}	zdyes ^{2}
bl**ee**zka ^{2}	napr**a**va ^{2}
vi, vas ^{2}	vsyo ^{2}
oozh**a**sniiy ^{2}	m**a**lyenkeeiy ^{2}
tooal**ye**ti ^{2} M (gents) Ж (ladies)	shyot ^{2}

2	2
it is possible	we want

2	2
here	tea

2	2
on the right	near

2	2
all, everything	you

2	2
small	terrible

2	2
bill	toilets

3 na	**3** av**to**boos(ye)
3 plakh**a**ya	**3** **p**ochta/**p**ochtoo почта
3 m**a**rkee	**3** nyelz**ya**
3 vsyo	**3** oonivyerm**a**g
3 magaz**ee**n/i	**3** atkriti
3 nyet prabl**ye**m	**3** koop**ee**t'

3	3
bus	on, by
3	**3**
post office	bad
3	**3**
it's not possible	stamps
3	**3**
department store	all, everything
3	**3**
open	shop/s
3	**3**
to buy	no problem!

3 shto	3 nyemn**o**zhka
3 gaz**ye**ta	3 vot
3 **ee**dyot	3 pag**o**da
4 kto-ta	4 pachem**oo**
4 n**o**myer	4 klee**ye**nt
4 kharash**o**	4 v**a**zhnaye

3 a little	**3** what/that
3 here is, here are	**3** newspaper
3 weather	**3** (he, she) it goes
4 why	**4** someone
4 client	**4** number
4 important	**4** good, well

4 kany**e**shna	**4** eentyer**ye**sna
4 kakd**a**	**4** spas**ee**ba balsh**oiy**
4 prast**oo**da	**4** vrach/vrach**a**
4 r**i**ba/r**i**boo	**4** beefsht**e**ks
4 p**ee**va	**4** stak**a**n
4 vad**a**/vad**i**	**4** neekt**o**

it is interesting	of course
thank you very much	when
doctor	cold
steak	fish
glass	beer
water	no one

5 vakz**al** вокзал	**5** ab**r**a**tna
5 p**o**yezd	**5** zapryesh**a**yetsa
5 m**a**la	**5** peesm**o**
5 pacht**o**viy **ya**shsheek	**5** **o**ba
5 p**ye**rvyiy	**5** p**o**lan
5 droog**oiy**	**5** **e**tat/**e**tee

5 back/return	**5** (railway) station
5 it is forbidden	**5** train
5 letter	**5** few, little
5 both	**5** post box
5 full	**5** first
5 this/these	**5** other, another

5 masheena	**5** staraya
5 astanovkye avtoboosa остановка	**5** glavnaiy ooleetse
5 byenzeena-pravachnaya stantseeya	**5** sotaviy tyelyefon
6 Razhdyestvo	**6** snyeg/snyegoo
6 payedyem	**6** tyeplakhod
6 S-SHA	**6** vyeleekalyepna

old **5**	car **5**
main street **5**	bus stop **5**
mobile telephone **5**	petrol station **5**
snow **6**	Christmas **6**
ship **6**	let's go **6**
great, wonderful **6**	USA **6**

6 chasta	**6** vnee**zoo**
6 aerapart**oo** аэропорт	**6** neechyev**o**
6 d**ye**tee	**6** m**a**lcheek
6 d**ye**vachaka	**6** z**a**vtra
6 neekakd**a** nye	**6** rad**ee**tyelee
6 droog/dr**oo**goo	**6** par**a**

downstairs **6**	often **6**
nothing **6**	airport **6**
boy **6**	children **6**
tomorrow **6**	(little) girl **6**
parents **6**	never **6**
it's time (to go) **6**	friend **6**

Myen**ya** zav**oo**t John. 1

Ya bil v **N**o**v**garadye. 1

pa b**ee**znyesoo 1

Oo myenya kvart**ee**ra. 1

Ya rab**o**tayu v **Lo**ndanye. 1

Oo nas s**in** ee doch. 1

Gdye vi rab**o**tayetye? 1

Mi **ye**dyem v Maskv**oo**. 1

Rab**o**ta khar**o**shaya. 1

Vi v **o**tpooskye? 1

My name is John. [1]

I was in Novgorod. [1]

on business [1]

I have a flat. [1]

I work in London. [1]

We have a son and a daughter. [1]

Where do you work? [1]

We are going to Moscow. [1]

The work is good. [1]

Are you on holiday? [1]

Oo vas est n**o**myer? 2

On nye rab**o**tayet. 2

Sk**o**l'ka st**o**eet? 2

S vasm**ee** do d**y**evyatee. 2

Eta sl**ee**shkam d**o**raga! 2

Mi khat**ee**m v N**o**vgarad. 2

Mi khat**ee**m bootyerbr**o**di. 2

Zdyes yest'…? 2

Gdye kaf**e**? 2

V kat**o**ram chas**oo**? 2

By you room? (Do you have…) ^2

He doesn't work (isn't working). ^2

How much costs (is it)? ^2

From eight until nine. ^2

This/it is too expensive! ^2

We want (to go) to Novgorod. ^2

We want (some) sandwiches. ^2

Here there is…? ^2

Where (is the) café? ^2

At what time? ^2

Syevodnya nam nada dyelat' pakoopkee. 3

Gdye zdyes avtoboos? 3

Golf nyelzya smatryet'. 3

Nam nada v bank. 3

Ya khachoo koopeet' footbolkoo. 3

Eta vsyo. 3

Gde zdyes magazeen soovyeneerav? 3

Magazeeni atkriti do kakova chasa? 3

Mi mnoga koopeelee. 3

Ochyen doraga stoeet. 3

Today for us it is necessary [3] (we must) (to) do shopping.

Where here bus? [3]

Golf it is not possible to watch. [3]

For us it is necessary (to go) [3] to bank.

I want to buy (a) T-shirt. [3]

That/it is all. [3]

Where here shop of souvenirs? [3]

Shops open until what time? [3]

We much (a lot) (have) bought. [3]

Very expensive costs. [3]

Kto-ta pazvan**ee**l. 4

On nye skaz**a**l, pachem**oo**. 4

Oo men**ya** sveed**a**neeye s neem. 4

Ya yev**o** zn**a**yu. 4

Tak nyel'z**ya**. 4

Shto vi khat**ee**tye peet'? 4

Shto vam? 4

Ochyen v**a**zhnaye d**ye**la. 4

Vi nye m**o**zhyete mnye pam**o**ch'? 4

Kak pa-r**oo**skee…? 4

Someone rang. [4]

He didn't say why. [4]

I have a meeting with him. [4]

I him know. [4]

One can't do that. [4]

What (do) you want to drink? [4]

What would you like? [4]

(A) very important matter. [4]

You couldn't help me, could you? [4]

How do you say… in Russian? [4]

Gdye vakz**al**? ⁵

K**akda** atkh**o**deet **p**oyezd? ⁵

Zdyes koor**ee**t' zapryesh**a**yetsa. ⁵

Do mooz**ye**ya dalyek**o**? ⁵

Zdyes yest' baln**ee**tsa? ⁵

Beel**ye**ti n**a**da prakampast**ee**ravat'. ⁵

Mnye ne nr**a**veetsa... ⁵

Taks**ee** nye d**o**raga st**o**eet, patam**oo** shta st**a**roye. ⁵

Gdye ma**ya** s**oo**mka? ⁵

Ya nad**ye**yus, shto prabl**ye**m nye b**oo**dyet. ⁵

Where (is the) station? ⁵

When leaves (the) train? ⁵

Here to smoke it is forbidden. ⁵

To the museum (it is) far? ⁵

Here there is (a) hospital? ⁵

Tickets it is necessary to punch (clip). ⁵

To me it is not pleasing (I don't like)… ⁵

(The) taxi not expensive costs, because (it is) old. ⁵

Where (is) my bag? ⁵

I hope, that problems there will not be. ⁵

V panyed**ye**lneek mnye **6**
na**da b**oo**dyet rab**o**tat'.

Ya nye mag**oo** zhdat'. **6**

Gdye vi zheev**yo**tye? **6**

Mnye n**a**da koop**ee**t' **6**
sotaviiy tyelyef**on**.

Oo nas m**a**lyenkaya kvart**ee**ra. **6**

Oozh**ye** kan**ye**ts n**a**shyeva **6**
otpooska.

Zdyes neechyev**o** **6**
padkhad**ya**shshyeva nyet.

V **e**tam gad**oo**… **6**

Kak dyel**a**? **6**

Da**ee**ytye, pazh**a**lusta, **6**
gaz**ye**too.

On Monday for me it
necessary will be to work. **6**

I can't wait. **6**

Where (do) you live? **6**

For me it is necessary to buy
(a) mobile telephone. **6**

By us (we have) (a) small flat. **6**

Already (it is the) end of
our holiday. **6**

Here nothing suitable there isn't
(There's nothing suitable here). **6**

This year… **6**

How things? (How are you?) **6**

Give (me), please,
(the/a) newspaper. **6**

*This is to certify
that*

. . . .

*has successfully completed
a six-week course of*

Instant Russian

with . . . . *results*

Date   *Instructor*

This is what readers think about *Teach Yourself Instant Languages* ...

'I am terrible with languages yet I am picking up Spanish! I found *Instant Spanish* excellent!'

Helen Goddard, Devon

'I was looking for a way to learn conversational French without all the vocab ... *Instant French* was just what I was looking for ... I found it very useful ... I found the Flash Cards extremely useful ... The way the chapters were designed made it interesting and fun ... I completed the course in 4^1/$_2$ weeks ... It inspired me to further my learning ...'

Christopher Preece, Aberdeenshire, Scotland

'We have completed your *Instant French*. We think it is wonderful.'

Tom and Maureen Peil, Preston

'Your little book will be used as a bible.'

Mr R.N. Turff, East Yorkshire

'I have always loved the French language but have been frozen with fear ... to actually use it ... (After Week 4) I had the confidence to use the telephone to book our hotel room – all down to you and your fabulous little book. Many, many thanks.'

Gary Hughes, Buckinghamshire

'... to say how delighted I am with your book *Instant Spanish*. You have made it easy to learn and fun with the flash cards.'

Sonia Frindt, Schönbrunn-Haag, Germany

'Seldom do I go on my woodland walks without my precious *Instant French*. It is in fact a course I can go over and over again and still learn more! ... J'ai 66 ans!'

Mr G. Rollings-Mathews, Kent

'Thank you for writing your book *Teach Yourself Instant Spanish*. I enjoyed its content, and its method and ease of learning. Over the past two years I have tried to learn Spanish by computer CD but it was just too difficult ...'

Mark Watkins (email)